PSHE and citizenship
AGES 7–9

Hilary Mason

CONTENTS

Author
Hilary Mason

Editor
Sarah Snashall

Assistant Editor
Simon Tomlin

Series designer
Lynne Joesbury

Designer
Rachael Hammond

Illustrations
Debbie Clark

Cover photograph
Getty One Stone

Published by Scholastic Ltd,
Villiers House,
Clarendon Avenue,
Leamington Spa,
Warwickshire
CV32 5PR
Printed by Bell & Bain Ltd, Glasgow
Text © Hilary Mason
© 2001
Scholastic Ltd
Visit our website at
www.scholastic.co.uk

4 5 6 7 8 9 0
4 5 6 7 8 9 0

British Library Cataloguing-in-Publication Data
A catalogue record for this book is available from
the British Library.

ISBN 0-439-01858-7

The right of Frances Mackay to be identified as the Author of this work has been asserted by her in
accordance with the Copyright, Designs and Patents Act 1988.

Introduction

This book suggests how PSHE and citizenship can be divided into manageable teaching units for seven- to nine-year-olds. Each themed chapter provides two units of work. These units are often complementary to each other and therefore you should choose one or other as appropriate to your needs. Most of the units can be used to form the basis of a substantial chunk of personal, social and health education work – perhaps over a half term – and by providing progressive lesson plans show how PSHE and citizenship can be sequenced. The grids at the beginning of each unit are intended to aid medium-term planning. They highlight (in bold) the enquiry questions covered by the lesson plans as well as additional enquiry questions which could be used to extend the unit further. The grids can also be used to help plan links that PSHE and citizenship has with other subjects across the curriculum, especially literacy and numeracy. (ICT links are given within the lesson plans themselves.) By providing a broad overview, the grids also help with planning the resources that you will need to collect in preparation for the unit.

The introductions to each unit provide some background information that you may find useful when working with the lesson plans. There is also guidance provided on matching learning opportunities to a range of ability levels.

Why is PSHE and citizenship important?

The second of the National Curriculum's two aims, states:

The school curriculum should aim to promote pupils' spiritual, moral, social and cultural development and prepare all pupils for the opportunities, reponsibilities and experiences of life.

Teaching PSHE and citizenship has a vital role in fulfilling this aim.

The importance of teaching children the skills and processes involved in becoming happy and fulfilled individuals in a healthy, supportive environment is increasingly being recognised. The guidelines for PSHE and citizenship have been developed and introduced partially as a result of serious concerns about the behaviour of young people and the breaking down of traditional sociological groups such as the family and local communities.

During the last five years the number of children and young people permanently excluded from school has reached record levels. The high numbers of children excluded from primary schools is cause for very serious concern. Youth crime is a permanent thorn in the flesh of government. Increasingly there is a realisation that it is the causes rather than the manifestations of crime that need to be addressed. Teaching children from an early age about why certain rules and conventions are necessary to protect the rights and freedoms of individuals is an essential first step in helping children to feel positive and make sensible decisions. Failure to internalise these lessons about how to live successfully in the family, in the local community and in the wider world inevitably leads to problems later on.

For too long what can be called the 'key life skills' have been left to develop in an ad hoc, unstructured way. Often we hope that somewhere along the line the children for whom we are responsible will just absorb what are actually quite complex skills.

PSHE and citizenship for seven- to nine-year-olds

This book aims to support teachers in helping children to develop the key skills involved in becoming healthy, positive and fulfilled individuals.

The philosophy upon which this book has been built reflects the aims of the National Curriculum (2000) non-statutory guidelines for PSHE and citizenship – and it also takes the themes a bit beyond the guidelines.

These guidelines suggest that during Key Stage 2 pupils should learn to take responsibility. This could begin with taking responsibility for their immediate environment by looking after the school grounds for example, or through creating a garden or wildlife area, recycling projects and so on.

The guidelines go on to suggest that children can also begin at this age to take responsibility for the needs of others, for looking after animals and for suggesting other, more environmentally friendly ways of getting to school.

The guidelines recognise that it is vitally important for the children to feel positive about themselves, to learn to recognise when they have achieved things and to celebrate that achievement. This feeling of self-worth is crucial for a healthy lifestyle.

Children should begin to understand at this stage something about the political processes that shape and affect our daily lives. There are activities throughout the chapters providing opportunities for the children to take part in democratic decision making, to decide how to support others less fortunate than themselves and to reflect upon some strategies for managing difficult situations and negative emotions. They are asked to find ways of resolving moral dilemmas and feelings of injustice.

Teaching PSHE and citizenship

Because teaching PSHE and citizenship deals with behaviour, feelings, decision making, one's place in society and other such abstract but critical concepts, it is very important to handle these activities with a great deal of sensitivity. Activities relating to family, friends, bullying, unfairness and so on can be difficult for some children to cope with. Children who have problematic home lives or behavioural difficulties will need to be supported and acknowledged and will generally cope best if taught in small groups or on a one-to-one basis.

However, just because something is difficult doesn't mean that it shouldn't be taught – indeed in this case the reverse is true. The skills and processes involved in learning to become fully

rounded independent people are so important that it is essential that they are taught – and taught in a safe, caring environment.

About this book

The chapters and units have all been developed from an overarching theme of 'building'. Beginning with the idea of learning how to build healthy relationships both at home and at school, the chapters progress through the themes of building healthy bodies, building and maintaining a healthy environment, healthy communities and moving into healthy futures.

Throughout the chapters, there is considerable emphasis on literacy and ICT, as well as links with other curriculum subjects, notably science. For each activity there is a list of suggested vocabulary and ideas for introducing the ideas to the whole class. Expected outcomes are listed at the end of each activity and also given in the grids.

The activities are structured so that teachers do not need to be experts on the many subjects covered by the book. There are clear guidelines for lesson development and plenary sessions.

Building healthy relationships

The guidelines state that children should 'develop the skills to be effective in relationships'. During the ages of seven to nine, the child's world is largely defined by school and by home. It is therefore vital that they have healthy relationships with peers and adults at school and with their family at home. These relationships are key to their sense of personal identity and well-being.

There are activities about how children see themselves and their personal history, what makes a good friend, how to deal with moods and emotions and what constitutes fairness and injustice. The activities reflect the underlying themes of the non-statutory guidelines, especially that: 'the children's actions affect themselves and others, to care about other people's feelings and try to see things from their points of view'.

Building healthy bodies

The non-statutory guidelines state that pupils 'should be taught what makes a healthy lifestyle, including the benefits of exercise and healthy eating, what affects mental health and how to make informed choices'. The overall aim of the activities in this chapter is to raise the children's awareness of healthy lifestyles and to demonstrate to them that they do have choices about their own diet and exercise levels. There are activities on understanding and choosing healthy foods and on the importance of exercise and of exercising safely.

Building healthy environments

Environmental issues have been somewhat edged out of the National Curriculum in recent years. And yet, children are often passionately interested in environmental projects on endangered species, conservation, alternative technology, pollution and recycling. The activities in this chapter give the children opportunities (as outlined in the guideline) to: take responsiblities, participate, make real choices and decisions, meet and talk with people, consider social dilemmas and find information and advice.

Building healthy communities

The guidelines state that pupils should be taught: 'Why and how rules and laws are made and enforced, why different rules are needed in different situations and how to take part in making and changing rules' and to 'recognise the role of voluntary, community and pressure groups'. The activities in this chapter look at the people that make up the school and local community around the children. The activities investigate the jobs people do in the community, the rules a community needs, the provisions various groups in the community need and voting.

Building a healthy future

A healthy future depends on two things – the kinds of decisions individuals make about how they want to conduct their lives, and sustainable development. Thus the two units in this chapter aim to develop the children's skills in making positive informed choices and also to alert them to the importance of managing the earth's natural resources. The activities ask children to think about the decision-making process itself – how does one actually make a choice?

Building healthy relationships

Building healthy relationships is one of the most important lessons we all need to learn in order to live happy, healthy lives. Relationship building begins from the moment we're born and continues right through our lives. During an average lifetime we make relationships of all kinds with a vast range of different people in a huge array of settings. These relationships begin in the family group, develop through friendships at school and extend into the local community and continue into our working lives. With some of these relationships there is a degree of personal choice, for example with a choice of friend or partner. Other relationships are 'forced' on us – we are powerless to choose a family into which we would like to be born, and young children have little say in choice of school, and we cannot always choose our boss.

Although relationship building is a hugely important process requiring quite complex skills, most of us have to randomly pick up these skills as we go along. For example, we learn from experience that if we shout at people they usually get angry or upset. It may take us longer to learn that creative listening is a much more effective tool than a raised voice.

No two relationships are ever the same – the way we relate to our GP is very different to the way we behave with our close friends for example, and what we choose to tell our best friends we may not want to tell our parents. However, there are certain generic skills involved in the process of building healthy relationships and these can be taught.

Key Stage 2 is the ideal age at which to begin the systematic teaching of the skills we all need to conduct our various relationships. Skills such as listening, reasoning, decision making and managing personal behaviour are key to the PSHE curriculum – and are such important skills that failing to master them can be a major barrier to learning.

It is for this reason that the activities in this chapter are all derived from questions and concepts based on these key life skills – what does it mean to be a good friend, what sort of person am I? How do I feel about my position in the family? How would we deal with someone who is jealous and so on?

During the ages of seven to nine, the child's world is largely defined by school and by home. Healthy relationships with peers and adults at school and at home are therefore vital to an individual's sense of personal identity and well being.

The themes and activities in this chapter are designed to introduce young learners to some of the basic concepts involved in building healthy relationships. One of the core aims of this chapter is to help build 'self-management' skills – the idea of taking responsibility for one's own actions. The first step in managing ourselves and measuring our behaviour is to know who we are – what makes us tick and what makes us angry, disappointed or frustrated?

The importance of understanding oneself is recognised in the National Curriculum non-statutory guidelines for PSHE and citizenship at Key Stage 2 which states: 'Pupils should be taught to recognise their worth as individuals by identifying positive things about themselves and their achievements, seeing their mistakes, making amends and setting personal goals'. It also states that children should be encouraged: 'to resolve differences by looking at alternatives, making decisions and explaining choices'.

Thus, there are activities about how children see themselves and their personal history, what makes a good friend, how to deal with moods and emotions and what constitutes fairness and injustice. The activities reflect the underlying themes of the non-statutory guidelines especially that: 'their actions affect themselves and others, to care about other people's feelings and try to see things from their points of view'.

My family

Clearly there are no hard and fast rules about what makes a good relationship and we all behave differently in a whole range of relationships. However, building healthy relationships is a key life skill and it is never too early for children to practise it. The first relationships we build take place at home, so it makes sense to start there. Mastering the skills and processes on which the activities in this unit build is the first step towards the children learning how to manage their own behaviour – something which is of increasing concern in schools across the country. The activities in this unit deal with the themes of:

● **knowing oneself in order to relate better to others**

In order for children of this age to understand what healthy relationships are and how to develop them, it helps if they try to understand something about themselves first. What makes them tick as individuals? What sorts of things make them happy or unhappy? What do they enjoy doing most with their family? How do they think other people see them?

● **understanding one's place in the family group**

Children often have quite strong views about their position in the family. Youngest children may aspire to being able to do the kinds of things their older siblings are allowed to do such as staying up later or going shopping with friends. Oldest children may feel protective towards their younger brothers or sisters or jealous and confused when a new baby is born into the family. It is important for the healthy development of relationships that children are given the opportunity to express these kinds of feelings. At this young age, it is sometimes difficult for children to communicate how they feel about themselves in the family setting. Exploring how and where they fit in to the family is a good beginning.

● **the different and individual personalities that make up the child's own family**

Family structures are often complex with many children experiencing the separation of their parents and the break up of the family. A proportion of your pupil intake will almost certainly be 'looked after' by the local authority in foster and residential care. For children such as these it is doubly important that they are given a safe environment in which to explore their feelings. There is a need therefore for great sensitivity around these children. For a small minority of children who have entrenched behavioural difficulties the activities in this unit will be most successful if they are conducted on a one-to-one or small group basis.

● **the idea of moods and their effect on others**

Young children can be quite self-absorbed and they need practise at considering the moods and needs of others. Giving them the opportunity to think about the special characteristics and personality traits of the people closest to them – generally their families – helps the children to understand that to get on well with others they need to take these special characteristics into account when they spend time together. At a simple level this can mean not shouting or running around grandma's house if she isn't feeling very well, or noticing when somebody is unhappy or worried. This is a fairly sophisticated concept for seven- to nine-year-olds, but at this stage they can engage with the general idea of what other people are actually like if the discussion and activities are kept simple and directly related to members of the children's own family.

● **the notion of fairness**

'It's not fair' must be one of the most frequently used expressions by children of this age – and also for many adults. Children often have an inflated sense of injustice and feel frustrated when they can't do something or have something they want. If children are not taught the necessary skills to manage these feelings of frustration and powerlessness they may become the disaffected young people who are problematic to teach once they transfer to secondary school. They may also 'act out' their sense of unfairness in inappropriate ways both inside and outside school. Although teachers naturally try to instil a sense of fair play in their classrooms, the children themselves need to internalise the messages and learn to understand why they can and can't do or have certain things at certain times.

UNIT: My family

Enquiry questions	Learning objectives	Teaching activities	Learning outcomes	Cross-curricular links
Who am I?	● Understand themselves as individuals. ● Reflect on how the behaviour of individuals can affect other people in the family group.	Read a story about feelings, discuss ideas and write a poem about who they believe themselves to be.	*Children:* ● identify own character traits ● understand that knowing oneself is an essential element of relationship building	English: sharing fiction; writing poetry; speaking and listening.
Where do I fit in my family?	● Gain a sense of personal history. ● Understand other family members by sharing stories and photographs.	Share and discuss family photographs. Class survey to investigate family positions. Make a graph from the data.	● understand that one's own position in the family may determine how we are treated	ICT: data-handling.
What can I tell you about my family?	● Reflect on the personalities of family members.	Share photographs and relate experiences in the family. Describe family members.	● understand what makes individuals special ● understand the needs of others	English: working with adjectives.
Are you tickled pink, seeing red or feeling blue?	● Understand that we all have different moods. ● Understand that our moods can affect others. ● Reflect on the ways our behaviour may affect other members of our family. ● Recognise the importance of body language.	Introductory work through a photocopiable sheet identifying body language. Practise body language through interpreting stance, expression and mood in pictures of people.	● are able to recognise body language ● understand that moods affect others around us	English: speaking and listening; using adjectives.
Is it fair?	● Reflect on the concept of fairness. ● Express considered opinions. ● Understand the reasons why they can't always do as they wish.	Teacher-led discussion to help establish what we mean by fairness. Small-group work on role-playing. Given scenarios.	● understand what fairness is and why certain things are 'allowed' ● are able to work co-operatively in a group	English: expressing views in a group. Drama: role-play.

Resources
A collection of story books that show how people feel about themselves (for example: *Angry Arthur*, by Hiawyn Oram; *Titch*, by Pat Hutchins; *Bill's New Frock*, by Anne Fine; *The Rainbow Fish*, by Marcus Pfister; *The Selfish Giant*, by Oscar Wilde); computers with word-processing software; newspaper/magazine articles depicting people in a range of moods; tape-recorders.

Display
Ask the children to bring in some family photographs, and enlarge them on a photocopier.

CHAPTER I
BUILDING HEALTHY RELATIONSHIPS

My family

Who am I?
1 hour

Learning objectives
• Understand themselves as individuals.
• Reflect on how the behaviour of individuals can affect other people in the family group.

Lesson organisation
Introductory discussion with the whole class followed by individual work.

Vocabulary
behaviour
character
personality
individuals
family
others

What you need and preparation

Gather together a collection of story books about how people feel about themselves, for example: *Angry Arthur* by Hiawyn Oram (Red Fox), *Titch* by Pat Hutchins (Red Fox), *Bill's New Frock* by Anne Fine (Mammoth), *The Rainbow Fish* by Marcus Pfister (North-South Books) and *The Selfish Giant* by Oscar Wilde (Puffin Books). Although the books listed here are written for a younger audience, they will also appeal across the age range and can help the children to focus on what makes a person tick. You will also need individual copies of photocopiable page 108. You may also wish to provide individual copies of photocopiable page 109 for the follow-up activity.

What to do

15 mins Introduction

Read your chosen story or stories to the whole class – perhaps as part of the Literacy Hour. Can the children recall and recount times when they felt the same way as some of the characters in the stories? Ask the children to compare how the characters behaved in the story with how they would have behaved in the same situation. Develop the discussion into a general class discussion about the sorts of things that make people angry or upset. How do the children feel when other people don't share things with them? How do they feel when members of their family get cross with them?

35 mins Development

Explain to the children that you would like them to write a short poem about themselves called 'I'm the sort of person who…' Give each child a copy of photocopiable page 108 – which contains the words of each line of a poem – and ask the children to fill in the end of each line. Encourage the children to be as truthful as possible.

When the children have completed their first drafts, read some of their poems to the rest of the class and ask them to guess who wrote it. With older or more mature children in the seven to nine age group, further discussion can be had about the differences between how individuals see themselves and how others see them.

10 mins Plenary

Recap on some of the characteristics described in the children's poems and discuss why it is important that the children understand something about themselves and why certain things trigger certain emotions in different members of their family – and in themselves. Discuss with the children how understanding themselves helps them to build healthy relationships with other people.

Differentiation

More able or older children could go on to write a second stanza for their poem. This stanza could either be about themselves or

another member of their family. For example, a second stanza could begin, 'My dad's the sort of person who…'

Less able or younger children could be provided with individual-specific vocabulary to help them write their poems. For example, for the line which begins, 'I'm the sort of person who imagines…', following discussions with the child you could write prompt words such as *castles*, *monsters*, *fairies* and so on.

Assessing learning outcomes

Are the children able to identify their own character traits and reflect them? Do the children have a clear sense of what they like and dislike and what makes them happy or upset? Can they explain why it is important to understand themselves in order to build healthy relationships with individual members of the family?

> **Follow up activity**
> ● Hand out copies of photocopiable page 109 and ask the children to fill them in. The purpose of this sheet is to reinforce the children's investigations into their own character, to help them to focus on their own strengths and weakness and to reflect on their proudest moments.

1 hour Where do I fit in my family?

What you need and preparation

Enlarge on a photocopier a handful of family photographs which the children should bring in to school a few days before you plan to carry out the activity. You will also need writing and drawing materials and access to a computer with word processing software.

What to do

20 mins Introduction

Display the photographs so that the whole class can see them. Ask the children whose photos they are to come out one by one to talk about them. Ask the children to talk about what was going on in the picture. How old were they at the time? What can they remember about the day the picture was taken?

Move the discussion along by asking who has brothers and sisters. Which children are the oldest and which are the youngest? How many children are there in the family?

Encourage a discussion about what it is like to be in a particular position in the family group. Is it something they think about? How do they feel about being older or younger than others in the family? What's the best thing about it? What's the worst thing?

30 mins Development

Carry out a class survey to investigate who is an oldest, youngest, middle child in families. How many children in the class are the oldest or youngest? What about only children – are they both youngest and oldest?

Help the children to set up a simple database on the computer. Have headings for the child's name, number of siblings and position in the family, for example oldest, second from youngest, middle. This will reinforce the concept of ordinal numbers and can therefore form part of the Numeracy Hour. It also introduces children to the idea of data handling and will reinforce aspects of ICT teaching.

Once you have demonstrated how to input information into the database, the children could work in pairs, taking turns to input their personal data about which position they occupy in the family. When all the data has been stored, the children could work with another class to collect more information about position in the family and make comparisons. Some children will be able to go on to make a graph of their findings.

> **Learning objectives**
> ● Understand where they fit in terms of age in their families in order to strengthen their sense of personal history.
> ● Share stories and photographs about their families to further their understanding of what sorts of characters they are.
>
> **Lesson organisation**
> Initial teacher-led discussion; whole-class activity; plenary.
>
> **Vocabulary**
> family
> characters
> oldest
> youngest
> siblings
> chronological

My family

Plenary
10 mins
Discuss some of the reflections children have made about their position in the family. Discuss some of the negative issues the children have raised, for example jealousy that their older siblings are allowed to do things they are not. Help them to understand the reasons why it isn't always safe or sensible for all family members to do the same things. What reasons can they think, for example, for why their parents would not let them go out with their friends on their own in the evening?

Differentiation
Less able or younger children could tackle the data handling aspects of this activity at a more basic level. They could, for example, draw pictures of the different members of their family showing where they themselves fit in. They can then label their drawings with captions saying, 'oldest, me, youngest', for example.

More able or older children could be encouraged to use the information from the database to draw conclusions. For example, they can find out from the data what the average family size is, or whether more children in the class have brothers or sisters. What percentage of children in the class has a brother/sister?

More able children could also be encouraged to investigate their family tree. This helps to give the children a sense of time and place.

Assessing learning outcomes
Can the children describe and reflect on their position in the family group? Can they describe members of their family to their classmates in a way that shows they understand why their position in the family may determine what they are and are not allowed to do?

(1 hour) What can I tell you about my family?

What you need and preparation

A few days before you plan to do the following activities, ask the children to bring in photographs of members of their families, including grandparents, cousins, aunts and uncles and so on. If possible they should bring in photographs showing one person only, as this helps them to focus on individual personality characteristics. You will also need writing materials.

What to do

(15 mins) Introduction

Ask the children to work in small groups. Invite the children to show their photographs to the rest of their group. Ask them to say three things about the person in the photograph. For example, 'This is my sister, Nikki. She is three years old. My sister loves pushing her little wheelbarrow round the garden.' Or, 'This is my grandad at the seaside. He went there after he came out of hospital. My grandad tells me lots of funny stories about when he was little.'

When the children have told the group three things about the person in the photograph, encourage the other children to ask questions to find out more about the person. For example, they might ask, 'How old is your grandad? How often do you see him? What does your grandad like to do best?'

To reinforce your literacy strategy activities, introduce the children to the idea of using adjectives to describe the key characteristics of their family members. Looking at some of the photographs again, ask the children to give three adjectives that describe something about the person in the picture. List their suggestions on the board or a flip chart. Encourage the children to think of interesting and colourful adjectives that portray something unique or special about that particular person. For example, 'humorous, moody, mischievous, jolly, gentle' and so on.

(30 mins) Development

Ask the children to choose one of their photographs and stick it in the middle of a piece of card or sturdy paper. Make sure they leave enough room to write adjectives to annotate the photograph. Make sure also that the photographs are not damaged in case parents/carers want them back. These can then be compiled into a class photograph album of the children's families. Can the children come up with a good title for the photograph album?

(15 mins) Plenary

Ask the children to consider what they think they have learned about their families and how individuals react to certain things. Why do they think it is important to consider what other people in the family are like as people?

Differentiation

Younger or less able children will gain more from the activities above if they are carried out as part of a small group – perhaps during the Literacy Hour – where they can more easily be supported to structure their thoughts and write the vocabulary.

Learning objectives
• Talk about their families and reflect on their individual personalities.

Lesson organisation
Group activity; individual activity; whole-class plenary.

Vocabulary
physical features
personality
individuals
consideration
understanding
respect

ICT opportunities
If you have the technology, it is possible to scan the photographs into a computer and print them out. The children could also use a computer to write the adjectives. They could then import the scanned photograph into the document with the adjectives. This has the added advantage of reducing the chance of the photographs being damaged.

My family

Older or more able children can compose pairs of adjectives to describe the special characteristics of the people shown in the photographs. They could experiment with rhyming couplets and build these into a poem.

Assessing learning outcomes

Can the children describe individual members of their family conveying what is special or unusual about them? Can the children show an understanding of why it is important to try and understand the character of other members of the family? Are they able to listen attentively to what other members of the group are saying? Can they speak clearly and hold the attention of the audience?

---

① hour Are you tickled pink, seeing red or feeling blue?

What you need and preparation

Collect some newspaper or magazine pictures depicting people in a range of moods. You will also need writing and drawing materials and photocopiable page 110. If possible arrange for the children to have access to a computer with an art program.

What to do

⑩ mins Introduction

Ask the children to work in pairs. Give each pair a copy of photocopiable page 110. Ask the children to discuss in their pairs what clues the character's body language give them about how they might be feeling. Explain to the children that what the characters are saying might not reflect how they are really feeling.

Let the children act out the emotions shown on the sheet. Ask for volunteers to demonstrate how they stand when they are angry or frightened. What sorts of facial expressions do they use when they are shocked, happy, worried etc? Let the children practise the use of body language by acting out the emotions shown on the sheet.

⑩ mins Development

Pin up the newspaper or magazine pictures so that all the children can see them easily. In turn ask the children to choose a picture and describe how they think that person was feeling at the time. What sort of mood do they think the people in the pictures were in when the picture was taken? How can they tell? What clues can the children detect from the body language of the people in the pictures – how were they sitting/standing, were they smiling or frowning and so on? Give the children an opportunity to 'mimic' the body language of some of the people in the pictures. Why might they have been feeling that way? Invite the children to relate a story about a time they felt in a similar mood to somebody in the pictures. Your discussion could revolve around how people behave when they are in certain moods.

How can you tell if somebody is worried or angry for example? What sorts of things do they do? You could ask the children to show how they might stand or look if they were happy or frightened and so on. This introduces them to the idea of body language and what this can tell us about what someone is really feeling – even if they are saying nothing. Steer the discussion towards the family and ask the children how their parents/carers, brothers and sisters behave when they are in different sorts of moods. Who would the children talk to if they were worried or upset about something? What sorts of things make various members of their family happy or fed-up?

My family

Familiarise the children with the cartoon strip format, making sure they understand that they read from left to right, as with text, and that the sequence of the frames is important if other people are to make sense of the story line.

Ask them to draw a three or four frame cartoon strip with captions and speech/thought bubbles depicting three different moods. The children could either draw the same character in three different moods or use three completely different characters for each of the three emotions. The children's contributions can be made into a wall frieze for the classroom or corridor. You can then refer to this in any future discussions about behaviour or if someone in the class is having a bad or especially good day.

If you have an art computer program, the children could import images of characters to use in their cartoon strips. They could also experiment with different types of font to write their captions and speech/thought bubbles.

10 mins Plenary

Discuss the children's cartoon strips even if they are not completely finished. Decide together where in the classroom to display the cartoon frieze when it is finished and agree that you will all try to remember that everyone has good and bad, happy or sad moods and these moods have to be taken into account in all relationships.

Differentiation

With younger or less able children you can ask them to use only two or three frames for their cartoons, perhaps giving them a visual prompt for the first frame. They can be supported to write less complex captions such as 'This is me in a silly mood', 'This is me in a grumpy mood' and so on.

Older or more able children can extend their cartoon strips into more frames or use more complex captions and subtle story lines. Ask them to try working with sayings that are about mood, for example 'feeling blue', 'seeing red' or 'tickled pink'.

Assessing learning outcomes

Do the children understand that people have a range of moods and feelings and that sometimes these feelings affect relationships? Do the children understand the idea of body language and how many hidden messages it can convey to others?

My family

① Is it fair?
hour

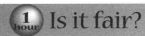

• Reflect on the concept of fairness.
• Express opinions on what sorts of things are fair and unfair.
• Understand that there may be good reasons why they can't always do the same things as other members of the family.

Lesson organisation
Initial whole-class discussion; activity in small groups; plenary.

Vocabulary
fair
unfair
equal
accept
angry
upset
communicate

What you need and preparation
Organise for the lesson to be held in a large space, for example in the school hall. You will need a tape recorder and writing materials.

What to do

⑮ Introduction
mins
Have an introductory discussion with the children to consider what they think 'being unfair' actually means. They may be able to give examples of unfairness in games, or when people don't take turns or say things about other people that aren't true. What kinds of things happen at home or at school that they consider to be unfair? Ask the children to say how they feel when they consider something is unfair – hurt, angry, upset or sad for example. Discuss what they can do when they think something is unfair – get cross, shout, talk to someone else about it, take some deep breaths, count to ten and so on.

㉟ Development
mins
Divide the children into small groups, ideally of three or four. Ask them to work together as a team to act out a sketch about something that is unfair. Encourage them to think carefully about not only the words they will say but also about the sorts of facial expressions and body language they will use to strengthen their points.

Once the groups have the bare bones of a sketch, ask them if they would like to act out their sketch to the rest of the class (the whole point will be missed if children feel compelled to perform in front of their friends. For the shy and retiring – it's not fair!) The other groups can offer constructive suggestions for making the sketch even better and could go on to suggest another 'scene' where the unfairness issue is resolved. They could suggest what the characters in the sketch could have done to be fairer.

If possible, give the groups another chance to polish up their sketches the next time you have a large space available.

⑩ Plenary
mins
Ask the children if they felt anything was unfair about the way the group worked out their sketch. Did everyone get a chance to have their say? Was anybody forced into doing something they didn't want to do? How did they resolve these problems and how could they avoid being unfair in similar situations at other times?

Round off the discussion by asking the children to think again about things they think are unfair at home, such as not being able to stay up after 8pm or go out in the evening with a friend like an older sibling may be allowed to. Can they think why parents/carers may not allow them to do certain things?

Differentiation

Younger or less able children may feel more confident acting out other story lines about unfairness using hand or finger puppets. They could perform these to younger classes in the school, perhaps during the Literacy Hour.

Older or more able children can produce quite sophisticated play scripts once they are shown how to set them out. Show them some play scripts if you possibly can – there's likely to be some in school left over from previous performances, pantomimes and so on. Discuss the layout and the importance of the dialogue and let them have a go for themselves.

Assessing learning outcomes

Can the children show that they understand what being unfair is about? Can they work fairly together in a group to produce a piece of work or solve a problem? Are the children able to express the reasons why they may not be allowed to do certain things until they get older?

Follow-up activity
Keep the children in the same groups and ask them to begin writing a short script for their sketch. Demonstrate on the board or a flip chart how scripts are set out (new line for each speaker, speech is preceded by the speaker's name). It isn't necessary for them to include stage directions or scene setting passages – unless they really want to.

ICT opportunities
Later, perhaps as part of literacy or ICT activities, the children could make a tape recording of their sketch.

Relationships
at school

Relationships at school

Friends are extremely important to children, just as they are for adults. At this age children tend to fall in and out of 'best friends' quite frequently. They may be devastated if they have a quarrel with someone they value highly as a friend, so much so that it can impede their learning. Equally, a pair of friends may not realise how excluding they are being to other children who may try unsuccessfully to share in their games and interests. Learning how to share their friends and work out problems for themselves within friendship groups is an essential skill if children are to develop supportive and healthy relationships. This unit covers the key themes that are considered central to good relationship building at school:

● **what makes a good friend?**
Helping children to identify the qualities and personality traits that make a good friend is an essential part of managing behaviour and finding friends who are supportive and positive.

● **jealousy**
Jealousy is part of the human condition. Children are easily aroused to jealousy and managing the feeling is an essential part of healthy friendships. Children of this age are apt to feel jealous, even possessive about their friendships. They often find it difficult when a close friend 'goes off' with someone else. This is the cause of many an argument and sometimes serious upset in the playground. The aim is to show children that it is perfectly understandable to feel jealous sometimes, but it is a negative and damaging feeling if left unchecked.

● **listening skills**
Listening is one of the most important elements in healthy relationships. Few friendships endure if the friends fail to listen to each other. In the pressure to achieve national targets for reading and writing, teaching children the skill of listening can be easily overlooked. As teachers we expect and train children to listen when we're talking or take turns when speaking and listening in a group. But is this really enough? Listening skills are complex. Sometimes we hear what someone is saying but we don't really want to join in; sometimes we pretend to listen – we appear to be listening but really we wish we were somewhere else. Active listening entails focusing on what the speaker is saying and wanting to build on from the ideas being expressed. The ultimate aim is to teach children how to be active listeners in their friendships.

● **bullying**
Bullying remains a serious problem in schools right across the age ranges. It features as a serious issue in a high number of school exclusions and school refusers. Unfortunately, most children will at some stage in their school lives be involved in bullying either as a victim, a perpetrator or as a support to a friend. Bullying takes many and various forms – from physical violence to more invidious types of behaviour, such as persistent, excluding individuals from playtime groups, racial taunts and emotional blackmail.

There is often a gap in our thinking as adults when it comes to deciding what actually constitutes bullying. Sometimes we are guilty of not taking the matter seriously enough when children try to tell us that they are being bullied. Sometimes, despite the best of intentions we can actually make things worse, for example by dealing with bullying behaviour in front of the rest of the class instead of somewhere in private. The crucial thing is to let the children tell you what they consider to be bullying behaviour, after all it is their everyday reality that matters.

● **the school as a multicultural environment**
Many schools have a rich multicultural mix and many children are bilingual, using English as an additional language. For some children, family members will speak little or no English. As is well known, this difficulty with communication can become a major barrier to healthy home-school relationships. When people can't understand what others are saying or writing to them they feel disempowered and alienated. The aim of these activities is to raise the children's awareness of how much they can learn from cultures other than their own, and to alert them to hidden prejudices towards 'difference'.

UNIT: Relationships at school

Enquiry questions	Learning objectives	Teaching activities	Learning outcomes	Cross-curricular links
What makes a good friend?	● Reflect on the qualities that make a good friend. ● Consider whether they themselves display the traits they most value in others.	Initial activity around a well-known story. Small-group exercises to define what makes a good friend. Agreeing a class priority order for friendship.	*Children:* ● express what makes a good friend and to reflect on their own attributes ● work collaboratively in a group	English: making lists; developing new vocabulary.
Do bullies rule OK?	● Discuss what bullying is and how it can hurt people. ● Begin the process of personal behaviour management.	Whole-class discussion. Small-group activity to begin building strategies for dealing with bullying.	● describe types of bullying behaviour and be aware of its impact on others ● recognise the need to manage their own behaviour	English: extended writing; shared writing.
Is everybody welcome?	● Consider how welcoming the school is to visitors. ● Multi-cultural awareness.	Whole-class introduction using 'Jabberwocky'. Small-group work to devise some strategies for welcoming visitors to school.	● become greater aware of the needs of others ● suggest practical ways for improving things	English: shared writing. Geography: working with the immediate environment.
Are you really listening?	● Explore the importance of creative listening in relationships. ● Practise listening skills.	Teacher reads a story to the class. Develop body language through practice. Further games and listening activities.	● understand the importance of listening well to others	English: reading; writing; speaking and listening.
Has anyone seen the green-eyed monster?	● Consider the impact of jealousy on relationships. ● Devise strategies for dealing with jealousy.	Share story of 'Snow White'. Paired work to plan a strategy based on a given scenario about jealousy.	● understand why jealousy can damage relationships ● work out strategies for dealing with jealousy.	English: shared reading; recalling a well-known story.

Resources
A collection of children's fiction about friendship (for example, *The Rainbow Fish*, by Marcus Pfister; *Winnie-the-Pooh*, by AA Milne), a board or flip chart, writing materials, *Not Now Bernard* by David McKee, a book or video of 'Snow White and the Seven Dwarfs', 'Jabberwocky' by Lewis Carroll.

⏱ 1 hour What makes a good friend?

Learning objectives
• Reflect on the qualities that make a good friend.
• Consider whether they themselves display the qualities they find most attractive in others.

Lesson organisation
Initial teacher-led discussion with the whole class; individual work; plenary.

Vocabulary
friendship
trust
qualities
sharing
humour
kindness
listening

What you need and preparation

Gather together a collection of children's fiction on the subject of friendship. These may have different themes such as sharing (for example *The Rainbow Fish*, by Marcus Pfister published by North-South Books) or friendship itself (*Winnie-the-Pooh* by AA Milne published by Heinemann).

What to do

🕐 20 mins Introduction

A good way to get into the subject of what makes a good friend is to read some of the many children's books that focus on the theme of friendship and sharing. For example the ever-popular *Winnie-the-Pooh* stories provide many opportunities to discuss how Christopher Robin and his friends worked together to solve problems, help each other and have fun. The children may also be able to relate stories about friendships from television programmes, films and videos they've watched.

Read one or more of the stories with the children. Ask them what they think the story was about. What did it tell them about friendship? How did the characters in the story take into account the personality of their friends?

Discuss with the children what they think are the qualities that make a good friend. What is it they like most about their own friends – their sense of humour, the fact that they share their games and sweets with them, because they are kind, gentle and so on? Ask the children to consider if their friends always show all of these special qualities or does it depend on their mood?

🕐 30 mins Development

Divide the children into groups of three or four. Ask each group to come up with a written list of six qualities they would look for in a friend. They should then number them in priority order with number one representing the quality they most value in a friend.

When the groups have compiled their priority list, invite them to read out their lists. Write their number one priority on the board or a flip chart. From this you can make a 'top ten' class list of friendship qualities.

This top ten list can later be made into a poster, perhaps using a computer. The finished product could be displayed in the classroom or elsewhere in the school for others to see.

To round off the lesson, ask the children to select one of the qualities identified as essential in a friend and write a short poem, story or play script that highlights that particular quality. For example, the children could write a few rhyming couples based on 'someone who shares' or a story about the day a friend cheered them up when they were feeling fed up or upset.

🕐 10 mins Plenary

Recap on the qualities the children have identified as being especially valuable in friendships. *What does it feel like when friends behave in a way you least expect?* Do the children think that they themselves have the qualities they like most in their friends?

Differentiation

With younger children you could carry out the activity as a whole class, reinforcing the written elements during the Literacy Hour.

Less able children or those who lack confidence in a group, will almost certainly tend to take a back seat during discussions. Such children will need additional encouragement and reassurance that their contribution is valuable.

Older or more able children can create further stories on the theme of friendship that they can then illustrate or use computer images from an art program to enhance their writing. They can also carry out an audit of literature in the class or school library of books written by well-known authors that focus on the theme of friendship. They can go on to choose their favourite and write a review to encourage a friend to read it.

Assessing learning outcomes

Can the children identify the qualities they consider make a good friend? Do they display these qualities towards their own friends? Can the children work collaboratively in a small group, taking account of the opinions of others?

Do bullies rule OK?

What you need and preparation

A board or a flip chart. You will also need writing materials.

What to do

15 mins Introduction

Introduce the subject of bullying to the whole class by asking them to think about all the different sorts of relationships they have in school – with teachers, lunchtime supervisors, classroom helpers and above all with other children. Encourage them to think about times when they have felt upset, hurt or angry in their relationships with others. Do they think bullying features in their relationships at school? Do they think the school is doing enough to resolve any bullying issues?

Ask the children to tell you what they think bullying actually is. What sort of behaviour do they think counts as bullying? Ask the children to talk about what they would do if they felt they were being bullied. Who would they talk to? Who would they prefer not to talk to and why? Record some of their ideas on the board or flip chart.

Learning objectives
• Discuss the problem of bullying and the effects it has on people and relationships.
• Identify what constitutes bullying behaviour.
• Introduce the concept of personal behaviour management.

Lesson organisation
Whole-class discussion; group work.

Vocabulary
bullying
victim
threat
intimidation
responsibility
support
understanding

Development

35 mins Divide the class into four mixed-gender groups, and tell them that they should think of themselves as members of an anti-bullying unit. Give each group a specific problem. Ask each group to:

● *Group 1* Agree on a definition of bullying. These definitions could contain a list of types of behaviour that they consider to constitute bullying.
● *Group 2* Agree on ways that bullies and those being bullied can be helped to change their behaviour. They should write down their suggestions.
● *Group 3* Come up with written suggestions to guide someone who feels they are being bullied. Which of these suggestions do they think would work best?
● *Group 4* Discuss and record five or six ways in which the whole school could do more to stop bullying.

Plenary

10 mins Call the class back together and discuss the groups' results. The definitions, guidance and recommendations can be drafted into a 'Dealing with Bullying Handbook' and displayed in the entrance hall.

Differentiation

This activity is of equal value to all children and they can all make a contribution to group discussions.

Older or more able children, or those with a particular aptitude for ICT can add case studies or incidents to the bullying handbook using a computer to enhance the visual impact of their work.

Assessing learning outcomes

Are the children able to identify different types of behaviour that in their view constitute bullying? Can the children demonstrate an awareness of the negative impact of bullying behaviour? Can the children demonstrate that they understand the importance of taking responsibility for their own behaviour?

Is everybody welcome?

What you need and preparation
Photocopiable page 111; writing materials.

What to do

10 mins Introduction
Tell the children that you have been thinking about how visitors feel when they come into the school. Do the children think it is a welcoming and friendly place to walk into? What sorts of things will visitors see as they first walk through the main doors? Would they feel comfortable and at ease or confused and anxious for example? Will they be able to read the notices on the walls or the pieces of writing on the display boards?

Give each child a copy of photocopiable page 111. Ask for volunteers to try and read it, or read it to them if they are reluctant to have a go, and ask them to try following the words as you read. How did they feel trying to read it? Ask the children to imagine how they would feel if they were faced with a piece of writing like this in the doctor's surgery or at a railway station. How do they think they would have felt if a piece of gibberish had greeted them on their first day at school?

30 mins Development
Divide the children into three groups and give each a specific task. Ask each group to:

● *Group 1* Come up with some written suggestions for ways the school could be made more welcoming to visitors who don't read or speak English very well. They might suggest things such as writing notices in Urdhu (Spanish, Chinese and so on), having an interpreter in school or writing letters home to parents in their mother tongue.

● *Group 2* Think of ways that the school could learn more from a range of cultures. For example, they might suggest inviting ethnic minorities into school to share stories and experiences from their birth country, or they might suggest learning simple greetings from a 'new' language to use during registration or for saying goodbye at the end of the afternoon.

● *Group 3* Carry out a multicultural audit on the class library. Ask the children to find as many books as possible in the time available that feature characters from cultures other than England.

10 mins Plenary
Ask each group to give a verbal report on their findings so that all the children are aware of the outcomes from each group.

Follow-up activity
The children could write a letter to
the school governors telling them
about their work on making the
school more welcoming and asking
them to help them put their
recommendations into practice.

Differentiation

Older or more able children can extend their audit of multicultural
books to include the school library or carry out a more extensive
review of your own class books. They can go on to look more closely
at how different races are portrayed in fiction and write a letter to
the publisher pointing out the shortfalls or praising the good points.

Assessing learning outcomes

Can the children engage with the subject and show an awareness of the range of cultures and
their particular needs in school? Can the children suggest practical ways of making the school
more welcoming to visitors? Can the children work collaboratively in a group showing empathy
and tolerance towards others?

(70 mins) Are you really listening?

**Learning
objectives**
• Practise listening
skills.
• Make the
connection
between good
listening skills and
relationship
building.
• See the impact of
body language on
communication.

**Lesson
organisation**
Teacher-led
introductory
session; a series of
short activities;
plenary.

What you need and preparation

A favourite or familiar children's story such as *Not Now Bernard*, by David McKee (Red Fox)
which is a classic on the theme of parents not really listening to their children. You will also
need writing and drawing materials.

What to do

(15 mins) Introduction

Read *Not Now Bernard* to the whole class. Ask them what was going on in the pictures.
Have the children understood that, essentially, the story is about how adults sometimes don't
really listen to what their children are saying. Read the story again to reinforce the messages –
what was Bernard actually trying to say? Why did his parents not hear him? Have they themselves
ever felt like Bernard? Ask the children to consider how well they think they listen – to their
friends, to you and their parents.

Vocabulary
listening
skill
active
focus
creative
supportive
communication

50 mins Development

The following short activities can be used to introduce the children to the process of active listening. They can be undertaken as a series of one-off activities and repeated intermittently through the term, or taken as a theme for a single lesson, perhaps as part of the literacy strategy.

● Ask for a volunteer to act out a short sketch with you for the rest of the class to observe carefully. Ask your volunteer to talk to you for two minutes about something that interests them such as a hobby, a pet or an ambition. It is a good idea, especially with the younger age group to ask your volunteer to think about what they will say the night before. Explain what you would like him/her to do tomorrow.

While your volunteer is talking to you (make sure everyone can see you both clearly) use the sort of body language that shows you are not really listening (looking around, fidgeting, not making eye contact nor nodding in agreement and so on).

At the end of the sketch ask the rest of the class to tell you if they thought you were listening carefully. How did they know? What sorts of body language gave the game away? How did the speaker feel at the time?

● Ask the children to work in pairs to have a go at a similar sort of sketch (as listed above) of their own. Some of the pairs could devise sketches showing the sorts of body language we use when we are really listening well (nodding in agreement, leaning in towards the speaker or adding words of encouragement such as 'really?' or 'that must be brilliant' and so on.)

● Have a 'class listening week' where everyday the whole class spends five minutes or so at the beginning and end of the day, not talking at all and just listening to the sounds that are all around them and that they generally don't notice. Try this both in the classroom and outside in the school grounds.

● Read the children a familiar or favourite story. As you read make several 'deliberate mistakes', such as changing the name of a character, changing locations or mispronouncing well-known words. Ask the children to raise their hands or clap when they spot a deliberate mistake. How many of these mistakes can they remember five minutes or an hour later?

● Give each child a piece of drawing paper folded in half. Ask them to write 'my friend listened when…' at the top of one side of the paper and 'I listened when my friend…' on the other. Ask them to draw or write and illustrate a short account appropriate to each heading.

5 mins Plenary

Recap with the children the reasons why it is important for friends to listen well to each other and how it feels to be 'unheard'. Remind them that their body language can speak volumes and that they should try to be really active listeners. Revisit *Not Now Bernard* to end on a humorous note.

Differentiation

With younger or less able children, focus more on the acting out and use of body language than on the writing so that their listening skills are not impeded by anxiety about the writing process.

Older and more able children may enjoy the challenge of scripting and rehearsing other sketches that portray characters variously pretending to listen or actually listening actively.

Assessing learning outcomes

Can the children recognise and use appropriate body language as a part of the listening process? Can the children focus and sustain their attention on the subject matter when someone is talking? Do the children understand the importance of listening well and the impact this can have on relationships?

75 mins Has anybody seen the green-eyed monster?

Learning objectives
• Think about and understand the effects of jealousy on relationships with friends.
• Devise strategies for dealing with feelings of jealousy.

Lesson organisation
Whole class introductory session; pairs or small group activity; plenary.

What you need and preparation

A version of 'Snow White and the Seven Dwarfs' in film or written form. You will also need enough copies of 112 cut in two for each pair to have one scenario between them.

What to do

25 mins Introduction

Tell, read or show the class 'Snow White and the Seven Dwarfs'. Discuss how the story deals with the idea of jealousy and what the consequences were. Explain that this is an extreme case of jealousy caused by the Queen's vanity and ask the children to talk about their own feelings of jealousy. How did they feel and why? What did they do about it? How was the problem resolved?

40 mins Development

Divide the children into pairs or small groups. Cut photocopiable page 112 into the two different scenarios and give each group a copy of one of them. It doesn't matter if more than one group has the same scenario.

Ask the children to discuss their group's scenario and work out what happened next. How do they think the characters dealt with the jealousy problem? Ask the children to act out the two frames. What sorts of words and body language can they use to depict feelings of jealousy? How can facial expressions be used to show jealousy?

If you have time, groups could work with more than one scenario. Ask them to focus their attention

on how jealousy can be resolved. What sorts of things can they do when somebody is being horrible because they're jealous? Ideas could include offering to share a new toy, game or friend with the person who's feeling jealous, or talking it over with the person concerned or another adult.

(10 mins) Plenary

Ask the groups to report back on their ideas and ask if they would like to act out their scenarios for the others to watch. Compare the different suggestions made by groups given the same scenario – how did they variously go about resolving the jealousy issue? Is there agreement about how jealousy can be dealt with? For example, the children may suggest that talking it over with the person concerned is a good strategy, or making sure they don't 'brag' when they have something new to show their friends. Recap on the feelings that are created when people feel jealous and how these feelings need to be managed in relationships. Ask the children to practise these skills with their friends.

Follow-up activity

The two-frame jealousy scenarios can be redrawn and drafted into a set of story boards on the theme of jealousy or made into a class story book for younger children.

ICT opportunities

Use a computer to draft the class jealousy story, along the lines suggested in the follow up activity above. Give the children the opportunity to edit their work and add designs, perhaps imported from a simple art program.

Those children who show particular aptitude or enthusiasm for ICT could also use a paint program to experiment with colour mixing to make colours that they feel represent jealousy.

Differentiation

Younger or less able children will enjoy retelling the story of 'Snow White', maybe using props or puppets to embellish their 'performance'. They can also try acting out other scenes about jealousy and writing words that are associated with feelings of jealousy such as *green*, *angry*, *hurt*, *left out* and so on.

Older or more able children can write other scenarios or make a new version of the Snow White story where this time the Queen is persuaded out of her jealousy of Snow White.

Assessing learning outcomes

Can the children describe how the emotion of jealousy is portrayed in a well-known story and relate such feelings to their own experiences? Can the children identify situations that might engender feelings of jealousy with their friends and can they suggest strategies for dealing with it?

Building healthy bodies

Heart disease is the biggest killer in Britain. Our death rates from heart disease are among the highest in the world. In the UK, in 1999, we spent £2.2 billion on 'salty snacks' – crisps, extruded corn snacks, tortilla chips and the like – and another £5.5 billion on sweets and chocolate. These statistics are undeniably related – yet somehow the 'healthier lifestyle' message isn't getting through. The recent National Diet and Nutrition Survey, commissioned by the Department of Health, found that most young people are not eating a balanced diet. The 'five portions of fruit and vegetables a day' message is being ignored. In fact most British children and young people are eating less than half this amount. One in five children between 4 and 18 ate no fruit at all in the week the survey was carried out. More worryingly, they are eating about one and a half times the recommended amount of sugar.

The survey also found that most young people over the age of seven are 'inactive'. The Health Education Authority recommends that young people take part in moderate intensity activity for at least an hour a day. However, a third of boys between 7 and 14 do not meet this target, and fewer than half of 14–18 year olds. Meanwhile the lack of fruit and vegetables in our diets contributes to coronary heart disease and some cancers. Young people may also be smoking and drinking alcohol, which exacerbate health problems.

The costs of poor diet to individuals in disease, discomfort and early death are very high, while the costs to society through the health services alone are growing all the time.

The two essential ingredients for healthy bodies are a balanced diet and adequate levels of physical exercise – which is what the two units in this chapter are all about.

The best hope of changing our current levels of unfitness is to help children understand the importance of eating well and taking lots of exercise. The lessons then need to be reinforced on a very regular basis until the children internalise them. They need to look first at their own personal lifestyles – to look at how much exercise they do during the course of a normal week for example, and monitor the sorts of food they eat. Children have only a limited amount of control over their diets as most of the food they eat is bought and prepared for them at home or at school. However, they can make choices about the snacks they eat or decide to eat the green vegetables rather than leaving them on the side of the plate. Asking their parents for fruit as a playtime snack instead of a chocolate bar is a healthier – and cheaper – option.

The overall aim of the activities in this chapter is to raise the children's awareness of healthy lifestyles and to demonstrate to them that they do have choices about their own diet and exercise levels. The activities also support the non-statutory guidelines on developing a healthy, safer lifestyle: 'Pupils should be taught what makes a healthy lifestyle, including the benefits of exercise and healthy eating, what affects mental health and how to make informed choices'.

The concept of healthy lifestyles links neatly across to other areas of the National Curriculum – notably Science and Literacy. There is an emphasis throughout the activities in this chapter on Literacy and, where appropriate, ICT. For example, many of the activities give suggestions for children's written work and presentations. They are asked to write poems, stories and short play scripts, make tape recordings, posters and charts. There is a list of relevant vocabulary at the beginning of each activity. These can be used to reinforce spelling and can be built up into a word bank for the children to use in their written tasks. In this way it may be possible for teachers to build the activities into the Literacy Hour.

Eating well

Teaching children about the importance of healthy eating, balanced diets and good nutrition has been part of the curriculum for a long time now. But still the British diet is infamous for being high in fats, salts and sugars, and low in fibre, fresh fruit and vegetables. As a nation we eat more than our fair share of junk food and have one of the highest rates of coronary illness in the world.

The aim of this unit is to raise the children's level of awareness about the food they eat. Of course, children do not always have control over what they eat, but they can learn the rudiments of healthy eating and begin to exercise some choice over the amount of sweets they eat, for example, or what they choose for lunch.

The activities in this unit, which can also be incorporated into your science and food technology curriculum, introduce children to the following themes:
● monitoring their own diet and understanding the need to aim for a balanced intake from the main food groups
● investigating the ingredients in recipes to assess their nutritional balance
● food hygiene
● reading and understanding food labels and being aware of artificial additives
● snack food and its nutritional value.

The activity outcomes will also reinforce work in literacy and numeracy, for example in reading and writing labels and menus and surveying and calculating ingredients and analysing data. The energy in food is measured in calories and joules and it may be appropriate to give children some opportunities to work out how many calories they eat per meal and find their average daily intake of calories.

A useful way of helping the children to understand the need to eat a healthy diet is to use the analogy of a car. Just as a car needs petrol to fuel the engine, the human body needs food to convert into energy to power its many and various activities. The body needs this energy for growing and moving, pumping blood around the body and for keeping warm. The children may be surprised that the body also needs energy when they are asleep. The amount of energy an individual needs depends on how active that person is. If more calories are taken than the body actually needs, they are changed into fat and stored for future use.

The children also need to understand that the food they eat is used to actually build the body. Skin, muscles, bones, the heart and all other organs are made and kept healthy by the food we eat.

All food contains one or more of six different substances: proteins, carbohydrates, fats, fibre, vitamins and minerals. A well balanced diet will have enough of each food substance to provide the energy the human body needs.

Today in the developed world there is an overwhelming choice and variety of food products in the supermarkets. We can buy exotic fruits and vegetables without travelling further than the supermarket and eat 'seasonal foods' like salad or strawberries at any time of the year. Although we have been adding substances to food for thousands of years to stop it decaying, convenience foods and the demand for certain tastes has led to an increased use of artificial food additives. Children being the consumers of the future need to be taught what to look for when they buy food and make informed choices about their diet.

UNIT: Eating well

Enquiry questions	Learning objectives	Teaching activities	Learning outcomes	Cross-curricular links
Are you eating a healthy diet?	• Know that diet is an essential part of a healthy lifestyle. • Identify the components of a healthy, balanced diet.	Teacher-led introduction about the importance of healthy eating. Small-group work on the main food groups. Research into the importance of balancing foods from different groups.	*Children:* • explain what a balanced diet is • understand that foods can be classified into groups	English: reading from a range of sources. ICT: surveys; collecting data.
Is this recipe good for you?	• Identify which recipes are well balanced. • Understand that food containing high levels of fat, sugar or salt should be eaten in moderation.	Work from a photocopiable sheet to investigate which is the healthiest recipe. Further research from recipe books to identify healthy foods. Discussion about how foods are cooked.	• understand and identify healthy recipes • understand the main food group classifications	Science: living things.
Is it clean, is it safe?	• Understand that bacteria and viruses are easily spread through food handling. • Establish safe, hygienic rules for handling food.	Discussion about sandwich making and the importance of good hygiene. Practical session to make sandwiches. Discussion on food shortage. Eat sandwiches!	• understand how bacteria can spread • observe the rules of good hygiene when preparing food	Science: health and safety; living things. English: writing a list of rules.
What's on a label?	• Understand the kind of information found on food packaging. • Introduce the concept of food additives and their effects on health.	Working from a display of packaging, read and understand the list of ingredients – including E numbers and additives. Group investigations to find out more about contents of food items.	• classify food into groups • recognise that some additives are 'artificial' and that some may be harmful	Science: classifying; healthy diets.
What's in a snack?	• Look for 'natural alternatives' to ingredients found in snacks. • Understand why eating too many of these foods is harmful.	Classify snack foods. Work from a photocopiable sheet to look for alternative foods.	• understand that high levels of fat, salt or sugar are harmful.	Science: classifying; healthy diets.

Resources
A collection of reference materials on food and healthy diets, recipe books, food wrap, airtight containers and snack food wrappers.

Are you eating a healthy diet?

1 hour

What you need and preparation

Gather together a collection of reference books on food and healthy diets. If possible, arrange for the children to have access to the Internet. You will also need copies of photocopiable page 113 and writing materials.

What to do

Introduction

10 mins Spend some time considering with the children the importance of a good diet. What do we mean by a 'good diet'? (In nutritional terms 'good' is generally taken to mean a balanced diet containing a range of foods from each of the main food groups – proteins, carbohydrates, dairy, fruit and vegetables and so on.)

Remind the children about the different food types that make up a balanced diet and discuss the range of foods which make up these groups – for example, dairy includes milk, cheese, yoghurt and so on while proteins come from fish, meat, pulses and so on. Establish the idea with the whole class that certain foods, if eaten to excess, are bad for us. These so called 'danger foods' include sweets, sugary drinks, salty snacks and fatty foods such as chips and burgers. It is important for their long-term health that children learn that eating too much fat, sugars and salt eventually damages the body's vital organs. The effect on the heart of too much fat is well known to cause the 'furring up' of the arteries – a bit like scaling on a kettle. Too much salt increases the risk of high blood pressure later in life.

Ask them what their favourite foods from each group are. Is there anyone in the class, or anyone they know, who doesn't eat food from a particular group, for example who doesn't eat dairy produce, who is a vegetarian, or who is allergic to wheat or gluten?

Development

40 mins Ask the children to work in small groups. Give each group a copy of photocopiable page 113. Explain that you would like them to list all the different foods they can think of under each category, for example under carbohydrates they could list bread, pasta, potatoes and so on.

Then give groups of children specific tasks as follows:

● Research, using reference books, CD-ROMs or the Internet, the nutritional importance of different food groups. Why, for example, is it important to eat plenty of fruit and vegetables? Why do we need carbohydrates?

● Research the effect of eating too much sugar in the diet. The children could be asked to look particularly at the effect of sugary foods and drinks on the teeth, or the relationship between fatty foods and the health of the heart for example.

● Carry out a class survey to find out how many times a week the children eat foods from certain food groups such as fatty burgers, fruit and vegetables and bread and so on.

Learning objectives
● Understand that diet is an essential part of maintaining a healthy body.
● Identify what makes a healthy, balanced diet.

Lesson organisation
Initial teacher-led discussion followed by a reinforcement activity; small group work; plenary.

Vocabulary
diet
nutrition
balance
carbohydrates
protein
dairy produce
vegetables
fruit

Eating well

ICT opportunities
● Ask the children to download information from the Internet relating to diet and nutrition.
● Ask the children to use the Internet to carry out more in-depth research into the nutritional importance of particular foods such as fruit and vegetables or fibre.
● Ask the children to use a desktop publishing package to produce healthy eating information sheets or leaflets to encourage others to eat a balanced diet.

● Plan and make a menu for a special celebration meal that has a good balance of foods from the different food groups.

(10 mins) Plenary
Gather the class back together and ask each group to report back on its findings. Ask them to say what they consider to be the most important finding so far, such as that the class eats a lot of fatty or sugary foods, or that sugar is found naturally in fruits (fructose).

Differentiation

Younger or less able children could work in small groups to make a large wall frieze showing different food groups. They can cut out pictures from old recipe books or magazines, stick them onto strong paper and add simple captions such as, 'We need calcium to make our teeth and bones strong'.

Older and more able children can carry out in-depth research into areas such as poor diets and the problem of malnutrition, different types of diet such as vegetarian, vegan, wheat or gluten-free and so on. These can then be added to the class information pack (see follow-up activity).

Assessing learning outcomes

Can the children identify the main food groups and explain why we need to balance our intake of foods from these groups? Can the children draw conclusions about their own diets and suggest ways of eating a more balanced diet – such as eating a piece of fruit or raw vegetables as a snack rather than sweets or junk food?

Follow-up activity
Discuss how your collective research into balanced diets could be made into a reference source for themselves and others to use later. This could be in the form of a 'We are what we eat' information pack or picture book to which they could later add further advice, leaflets and recipes and so on.

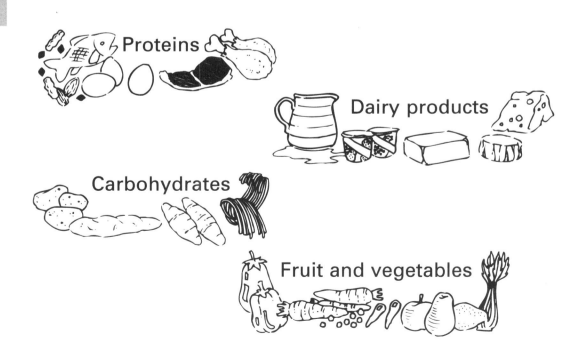

Proteins

Dairy products

Carbohydrates

Fruit and vegetables

Is this recipe good for you?

What you need and preparation

A few days before you plan to carry out this activity, ask the children to bring in unwanted recipe books (that can be cut up) or recipes from magazines. The children could also ask the school cook if she/he has any spare recipes of favourite school dinners that you could borrow for a couple of days. You will also need copies of photocopiable page 114 and writing materials.

You could carry out this activity as a natural follow on from the previous one 'Are you eating a healthy diet?' Alternatively it will work just as well on its own.

What to do

Introduction
15 mins

Introduce the activity to the whole class, explaining that you would like them to investigate recipes to find out which ones are well balanced and which ones are too high in certain foods such as fat or sugar or salt.

Remind them of the different food groups into which food can be classified.

Divide the children into small groups or pairs. Give each pair or group a copy of photocopiable page 114. Read the sheet through with the whole class to make sure they understand what it is they should be looking for when trying to decide which is the 'healthiest' recipe. Ask the children to investigate which recipe uses the most fat (butter, oil, margarine), sugar or salt.

Development
35 mins

As the groups finish their worksheets, give them two or three recipes from your collection to work with. Tell the children that you would like them to look carefully at the list of ingredients for each recipe and arrange them into different food groups. For example, the ingredients for spaghetti bolognese could be grouped into proteins (meat and cheese), carbohydrates (pasta), fruit (tomatoes) and fat (olive oil).

When they have completed their classifications, ask the children to write two or three sentences explaining which of their recipes are most balanced and which are not. Call the class back together and ask the children to think about what method of cooking their recipes used – baking, grilling, frying, sauté and so on. What can the children tell you about these different cooking methods? Which do they think are the healthiest/ least healthy methods and why?

Plenary
10 mins

Bring the class back together and discuss each group's findings. How many of the recipes are well balanced? How many of the dishes should they eat only occasionally?

Learning objectives
• Investigate which recipes are healthy and well balanced.
• Understand that if dishes are particularly high in fats or sugars, for example, they should only be eaten occasionally.

Lesson organisation
Initial teacher-led discussion reinforced by a worksheet; small group work; plenary.

Vocabulary
recipe
ingredients
fat
sugar
salt

Eating well

ICT opportunities
If you have the facilities and the time, children can make a simple database on the computer recording which popular foods are high in ingredients from particular food groups, for example bananas are high in vitamin C and fibre. Or which foods we can eat as much of as we like, such as fruit and vegetables, and which we should eat in moderation such as carbohydrates, saturated fats, sweets or fizzy drinks.

Follow-up activity
The results of the children's research and ideas can be collated into a 'recipes for healthy living' cookbook, which could be sold at the school fair.

Differentiation

Younger children may enjoy setting up a café in part of the classroom and using it for role-play. Their café should have a healthy eating theme and will only offer dishes that are well balanced and healthy. The children can prepare a menu board for the wall or window of the café by drawing or cutting out pictures of healthy dishes and writing simple captions for them, for example, 'low-sugar puddings', or 'the perfect low-fat starter'.

Older and more able children can plan a week's menus for somebody who is recovering from an illness and who therefore needs an especially 'good diet', for example one which is high in vitamins and low in fat.

Assessing learning outcomes

Can the children work out which of the two recipes given on the worksheet is the healthiest and say why? Can the children classify recipe ingredients into the main food groups and say why some recipes are especially well balanced, or too high in 'danger foods' such as sugar, salt or fat?

① hour Is it clean, is it safe?

Learning objectives
• Understand that bacteria and viruses can easily be spread through food handling and that simple, safe routines can reduce their spread.

Lesson organisation
Initial teacher-led introduction; individual, practical activity with support from classroom helpers; plenary.

Vocabulary
hygiene
bacteria
microbes
allergies
virus
disease
salmonella

What you need and preparation

The day before the lesson, ask the children to bring in the next day two slices of bread and the ingredients for their favourite sandwich filling. Have some spare ingredients and bread for those children who are unable to bring ingredients from home. Organise the support of a classroom helper, or helpers such as older children, parents, support assistants and so on for the lesson. You will also need some food wrap or airtight containers and a board or flip chart.

What to do

⑩ mins Introduction

Explain to the children that they are going to make some sandwiches to eat as a treat at the end of the school day. Talk to them about the importance of food hygiene and how easily bacteria on food (microbes) can be transferred and disease spread. You could ask them if they know what salmonella is for example, and where they have heard about it. Ask them to recap on the sorts of things they should always do when handling food, for example washing their hands, making sure surfaces and equipment are clean, not putting their hands in their mouth while working with food, keeping food cool and so on.

Write these 'food hygiene golden rules' on the board or flip chart.

㉟ mins Development

With the support of classroom helpers if appropriate (generally with the younger children), help the children to make their sandwiches during the afternoon. Recall the discussion you had earlier in the day about the importance of food hygiene, and make sure they can all see the board or flip chart containing your 'food hygiene golden rules'. Tell the children they have to cover the sandwiches and leave them in a cool place in the classroom (or a fridge if you have easy access to one). Ask the children to tell you why they think it is important to cover food if it is made in advance. What do they think will happen to their sandwiches if they are left uncovered? Do they think they will necessarily be able to see if anything is damaging/endangering the bread or fillings?

Ask the children to make a label for their sandwiches. Depending on the age and ability of the children, their labels could include, for example, a list of ingredients and their nutritional value, any special warnings or information for people following special diets due to allergies, religion, beliefs and so on. For example the labels could say 'this sandwich contains nuts', 'this sandwich is suitable for vegetarians' or 'this sandwich contains pork'.

Leave one of the sandwiches uncovered in a warm place in the classroom. Keep one sandwich wrapped in cling film and leave it next to the uncovered sandwich. Tell the children they should not touch the uncovered sandwich without asking first and that if they do handle it they must wash their hands carefully afterwards. During the course of the next five days ask the children to monitor what happens to the two sandwiches. Their observations can be recorded as a written chart or entered into a database using a computer.

Plenary

15 mins Enjoy eating the sandwiches at the end of the day.

Make sure there is nobody with food allergies such as to nuts, dairy produce or wheat who should not eat certain sandwiches. Remind the children to wash their hands before they eat and ask them why it is so important to do so.

Differentiation

With older children you can ask them to make a more complicated dish involving some cooking such as a pasta dish, a pizza or cakes. They can produce more comprehensive labels for their dishes including recommendations for a side dish or accompaniment for example, 'this dish is delicious if served with yoghurt and honey'. Or they can produce a more detailed analysis of the nutritional value of the ingredients for example, 'this dish provides you with half the amount of fruit and vegetables you need to eat everyday as part of a balanced diet', or, 'this dish should be eaten within two days. Uneaten portions should be covered and stored in the fridge', 'Do not freeze' and so on.

Assessing learning outcomes

Do the children understand the need to observe the rules of good hygiene when preparing and eating food? Do they understand that microbes that contain harmful bacteria are easily spread from food to person and vice versa?

ICT opportunities
Using a computer, the children can make the 'golden rules for food hygiene' list that you drew up at the beginning of the lesson into a useful resource for the classroom or kitchen at home. This could be illustrated using an art programme or with the children's own drawings.

Eating well

1 hour What's on a label?

Learning objectives
• Recognise the importance of reading food labels and packaging as part of maintaining a healthy diet.
• Understand how food-labelling works, especially the fact that ingredients are listed in order according to quantities used.
• Become aware of the concept of food additives and their effects on health.

Lesson organisation
Whole-class, teacher-led discussion; small group work; plenary.

Vocabulary
preservatives
additives
E numbers
substances
chemicals
sodium
natural
artificial

What you need and preparation
A couple of days before you plan to do this activity ask the children to bring in from home some empty food cartons, cans and packets and so on.

What to do

20 mins Introduction
Make a display collection of the packets and invite the children to sort and arrange them in different ways for example, into sweets, savouries, snacks, organic and so on. With the whole class, or in small groups if this suits your classroom organisation better, read the ingredients listed on the labels. Talk about how many ingredients it often takes to make something simple like a bar of chocolate or a breakfast cereal. Are the children surprised by any of the ingredients – did they expect, for example, there to be salt in Weetabix or starch in custard powder? Establish that on food labels, ingredients are listed in order of amounts used – the ingredient that there is most of in the product is the first one listed.

Are there any ingredients or substances that the children don't recognise such as preservatives, monosodium glutamate, dextrose saccharin and so on? Explain that these are called 'artificial additives' which are usually chemical substances added to foods to stop them from going off (preservatives) or to add flavour (for example, monosodium glutamate) or to give added sweetness (saccharin).

Draw the children's attention to any E numbers or additives listed in the ingredients. Explain that these are sometimes natural substances such as pectin to help set jam or carotene to add colour, but they are often made from artificial chemicals. Talk to the children about why these extra ingredients are added (to enhance flavour or colour, to preserve the food for longer and so on). Explain that if these chemicals are eaten in too high a quantity they may damage our health.

30 mins Development
Divide the class into groups of four or five children. Give each group a collection of empty food packaging. Ask each group to investigate a specific issue as follows:
● *Group 1* Use the collection of food packaging to find out and record which of the foods have the greatest/smallest number of ingredients.
● *Group 2* Devise a way of classifying the packaging. Examples of sets could include savouries, sweets, cereal, fruit, vegetable and so on.
● *Group 3* Find from the packaging the product with the highest amount of E numbers. List the numbers under the name of the product.
● *Group 4* Research which food products from the collection of packaging in front of them contain salt (sodium). Do any products list salt as amongst the highest ingredients (for example where salt is listed as the first, second or third major ingredient)?

Eating well

● *Group 5* Research which products from the packaging given contain ingredients that could be dangerous for people with food allergies such as nuts, wheat, gluten or dairy products. Does the packaging carry any warnings for such people?

10 mins Plenary

Ask each group to report back on its findings and give the rest of the class a chance to ask questions or make positive suggestions for finding out more about the subjects. Did anything surprise them?

Discuss who would find it useful to know about the sorts of things they have found out – parents, professional cooks, shopkeepers and so on.

Differentiation

Older or more able children could extend their investigations to find out more about E numbers and food additives. Are they necessarily all bad for us? How did people keep food from going off before the use of artificial preservatives and the invention of the refrigerator? They can also investigate the effects of excess salt on the heart and circulatory system or the importance of sugar levels for diabetics.

Younger and less able children may find it easier to work in larger scale. For example, to help them understand the concept of sets and food types, you could give them hoops from the PE cupboard and they could physically place their food packaging into the appropriately labelled hoop. Alternatively they could make a large collage picture of food products and their lists of ingredients.

Assessing learning outcomes

Can the children use food labels and packaging to classify foods into groups according to agreed criteria, for example savoury, fruit, vegetables and so on? Can they show that they recognise the importance of reading the labels on food packaging? Can the children identify the artificial additives on food labels and give reasons why we should avoid consuming too many of them?

Follow-up activity
Discuss with the whole class how they could most effectively share some of the things they have discovered about food labels and additives with other people. For example would it make a good article for a newspaper or food column? Or would their findings be useful as a booklet to put in a doctor's or dentist's surgery?

Eating well

(55 mins) What's in a snack?

Learning objectives
• Understand that snack foods contain ingredients that can be found more naturally in other foods – such as sugar from fruit.
• Understand that we need to be careful about the amount of snack or junk food we eat as these tend to be high in fats, sugar, salt and artificial additives.

Lesson organisation
Initial, teacher-led discussion with the whole class; short, individual reinforcement activity using the worksheet; small group work; plenary.

Vocabulary
snack
nutrients
alternative
natural
substances
additives

What you need and preparation

Gather together snack food wrappers such as crisp packets and chocolate, sweet and biscuit wrappers. Alternatively you could ask the children to use the wrappings from their lunch boxes. Make available a collection of reference books on nutrition, healthy eating, fast food restaurants and so on. You will also need copies of photocopiable page 115 and writing materials.

What to do

(15 mins) Introduction

With the class, read the ingredients listed on a few of the snack food wrappers. Discuss with them the fact that we eat a lot of snack or junk foods. If possible, give the children some statistics about how much snack food we eat. (For example, in Britain during 1999, we spent £2.2 billion on salty snacks, and another £5.5 billion on sweets and chocolate.) When do the children eat these kinds of foods? When do they most want to eat them? Explain that we tend to want to eat snack foods when we are really hungry and feel that we need to eat something immediately. Establish with the children that these kinds of foods are fine to eat occasionally but if we eat too many of them they are bad for us – this is because they are generally high in sugar, saturated fat, artificial additives, salt and so on.

Tell the children that many of the ingredients and nutrients in snack foods can be found in other, more natural foods. For example a packet of plain crisps contains potatoes, oil and salt which can be eaten in purer, more nutritionally balanced foods such as baked or boiled potatoes and oil in salad dressing. We don't need the salt in this form at all.

(30 mins) Development

Give each child a copy of photocopiable page 115 and take the children through the first example, which has been done for them. Tell them to fill in the boxes for the chocolate bar and the fizzy drink.

Ask the children to work in pairs or small groups. Give each group two snack food wrappers and ask them to list the ingredients on their wrappers and to find out some alternative, more natural sources for these ingredients. Ask them to fill in their findings in the boxes on the sheet. The obvious example is sugar, which is found naturally in fruit. Encourage the children

to use the reference books or the Internet to research if appropriate. Can the children identify which ingredients are not found in other, natural foods? An example could be a chemical additive (E numbers) or a main ingredient such as a tomato.

Plenary

10 mins Bring the class back together, even if they have not yet completed their task. Discuss each group's findings and ideas and invite the rest of the children to suggest other sources for particular ingredients and nutrients. Draw the children's attention to some of the gaps they will inevitably have in their 'natural sources' column. For example, they may not have found alternative or natural sources for some of the E numbers or chemicals. Ask the children why they think these substances have been added (to enhance colour and flavour or to preserve the product for longer).

Differentiation

Give younger or less able children wrappers that have a short, simple list of ingredients such as crisps or peanuts and raisins. They will find the words easier to read and the amount of information easier to manage.

Older or more able children can carry out further research on particular nutritional components such as vitamins, minerals, fibre and so on. These children could also make their own version of the worksheet or invent a snack/whole food snap game by sticking a snack food wrapper on one piece of card and alternative sources on the other. For example they might stick a crisp packet (or part of one) on one card and a picture (cut out or drawn) with potatoes, salt and oil on another card. The children make several sets of cards like this, shuffle them up and play 'snack snap' with them.

Assessing learning outcomes

Can the children identify the ingredients on the snack food labels and identify alternative, more natural sources for these ingredients? Can they make deductions about why there are no obvious alternatives for some of these ingredients?

Keeping fit

There is increasing concern about the levels of exercise taken by children in this country, and several studies have revealed that many children exercise much less than they should for the development of good long-term health. Alongside this is a concern over high levels of obesity amongst school-aged children and the effects that this has not only on their bodies but also on their learning and emotional well-being.

There are many reasons why children may take insufficient exercise. Many parents are concerned about the dangers from cars and strangers when children play outside; an increasingly mobile and geographically widespread school population leads to fewer children walking or cycling to school; and the enticement of television and computers and the pressures of a full school curriculum squeeze the time available for sport and exercise. Children may not have control over some of these factors, such as how far away from the school they live, but even at this young age they can be taught to reflect on their levels of exercise and have some choice about how active they are.

The activities in this unit look at the following themes:

● **monitoring personal exercise levels**

Children may not realise how little exercise they have during the course of a week – others of course will be exercising a great deal. Asking the children to monitor their activities and helping them to plan their time effectively is the first step towards keeping fit.

● **joining an exercise club**

When we talk of exercise most people think of gymnasiums, fitness clubs or team sports. There are opportunities within this unit for teaching the children how to go about joining a club. There are also many other forms of exercise that we may not even realise we're doing – running up and down the stairs, mowing the lawn, digging the garden. These are easy for most children to do at home and they are encouraged here to incorporate these types of activities into their weekly timetables.

● **the dangers of exercising incorrectly**

It is very important that from an early age children are taught the importance of warming up the muscles before beginning any form of vigorous exercise. They need to understand that failing to do this can lead to serious injury later on in life – especially the overuse of certain muscles such as those used for throwing, stretching and playing racket games such as tennis or badminton. Children also need to understand that exercising directly after a meal can lead to stomach cramps and also that if they are recovering from an illness they need to take moderate exercise at first while the body is repairing itself.

● **the body's response to exercise**

To help the children understand what happens to their bodies during exercise this unit also contains ideas for the children to learn about how muscles and joints work, how the heart and lungs respond before, during and after exercise. These activities also reinforce the children's research skills.

● **inventing a game to promote exercise**

The final activity invites the children to invent their own games based on what they have learned about the body and exercise.

UNIT: Keeping fit

Enquiry questions	Learning objectives	Teaching activities	Learning outcomes	Cross-curricular links
Exercise – how much is enough?	• Identify levels of exercise. • Understand that there are many different forms of exercise. • Make the links between exercise and health.	Introduction to the whole class through pictures of famous sportsmen and women. Fill in timetables to plan exercise.	*Children:* • assess levels of personal exercise • design and organise timetables to record when exercise can be taken	PE: health and fitness; exercising and the heart. Science: living things.
Have you joined in and joined up?	• Learn how to join a fitness club or group. • Assess which club and activities to get involved in.	Introduction through discussing a collection of promotional literature. Small-group investigations to find out about local groups.	• know how to join a club • understand why clubs advertise	ICT: research using the Internet. Numeracy: investigating costs and money.
Can exercise hurt you?	• Identify the dangers of exercising incorrectly. • List some dos and don'ts of correct exercise procedures.	Introduction to whole class then the children begin to identify dos and don'ts through a photocopiable sheet. Collation of ideas into a poster.	• understand the importance of warming up before vigorous exercise • recognise the sorts of problems that may occur if guidance isn't followed	PE: warming up before exercise. ICT: designing a poster Science: the human body.
What happens to your body when you exercise?	• Understand what happens to different parts of the body during exercise. • Locate and name parts of the body and research the effects of exercise upon them.	Introductory teacher input on joints, muscles and bones. Small-group investigations.	• locate heart, lungs, pulse, muscles and limbs • identify changes to the body during exercise	Science: the human body. PE: stretching muscle groups. Numeracy: measuring pulse rates.
Can you invent your own games?	• Invent games to encourage others to take more exercise. • Compare the sorts of games it is possible to play in different seasons. • Understand the needs of disabled people.	Introductory discussion. Group work to invent new games for different seasons.	• understand the needs of disabled people.	

Resources
Reference books on sport and exercise, leaflets and posters from a local leisure centre, an enlarged map of the local area, a local directory of yellow Pages, reference material on muscles and joints, sopwatches, balloons, pictures from magazines on the Paralympics.

Display
Pictures of famous sporting personalities.

① hour Exercise – how much is enough?

Learning
objectives
• Identify how
much exercise they
do during the
course of a normal
week.
• Understand that
exercise comes in
many different
forms – not just
from sport.
• Understand the
links between
exercise and
health.

Lesson
organisation
Initial whole-class
discussion;
individual work;
plenary.

Vocabulary
exercise
fitness
time-management
leisure
Olympics
special needs
disability

What you need and preparation

Gather together pictures of famous sporting personalities such as Olympic athletes, marathon runners, swimmers, football players and so on. These can be collected from newspapers, magazines and reference books. Collect together some reference books on sport and exercise. You will also need copies of photocopiable page 116.

What to do

15 mins Introduction

Introduce the subject of exercise and its central importance to healthy living by looking at the pictures of famous sportsmen and women. Ask the children to think about how fit these people must have to be to compete at this level and how much exercise they have to do each week in order to stay at the peak of fitness. Talk about the fact that Olympic athletes, for example, train for four years to reach their peak fitness and that they often exercise for more hours a day than the children are in school. Ask the children if it would be practical for the rest of us to exercise that much. How could we fit everything into a day? How much exercise do the children do – in school, in their spare time, or as a member of a club and so on? Remind them that it isn't only sport and team games that provide exercise, but also things like walking to school, helping parents in the house and garden, running errands and so on. Explain to the children that exercise is essential if we are to keep our bodies in good condition, even if we're not Olympic athletes.

40 mins Development

Ask the children to make a list of all the different forms of exercise they take during the course of a normal week. They can write their list as two columns, one headed 'at home' and the other 'at school'. The 'at home' column should include exercise taken at clubs such as swimming or tennis and so on, as well as other, less obvious forms of exercise such as helping to dig the garden, mow the lawn or running up and down the stairs to help with the chores.

After about 15 minutes when they have a basic list, bring the class back together to discuss

how many times a week they exercise and what forms this exercise takes. Discuss with the children which forms of exercise are particularly beneficial – helping with the vacuum cleaning is a good form of gentle exercise for stretching and bending but it doesn't provide much exercise for the heart. The sort of exercise that is most beneficial is that which makes you slightly breathless – such as brisk walking, running or playing a game like football or tennis.

Give each child a copy of photocopiable page 116. Ask them to use their timetable plan their weekly exercise. How are they going to fit in all the tasks that they have listed in their columns? Explain that they need to plan their week to ensure that they get maximum exercise whilst also managing all their other activities and commitments – such as doing homework, watching TV or playing with friends.

5 mins Plenary
Discuss the children's ideas for a healthy exercise timetable and talk about how they can achieve this – will they join more clubs, spend less time playing computer games, walk to school instead of getting a lift in the car and so on?

Differentiation
The amount of control the children can actually have over their exercise regimes depends to some extent on the age of the children and their access to facilities. But they can all exercise more in ways that are not always immediately apparent to them such as by helping in the garden or by doing some housework instead of watching TV for long periods over the weekend.

Older and more able children can carry out a class survey to investigate how much they actually exercise and express the data according to the amount of hours spent exercising, the types of exercise done and so on. They can then draw conclusions, for example about whether the amount of exercise done increases or decreases on a Saturday and Sunday.

Assessing learning outcomes
Can the children identify and record how much exercise they do during the course of a week and suggest ways of taking responsibility for increasing the amount of exercise they do? Can the children show how they can fit in exercise on a regular, weekly basis?

ICT opportunities
The children could make a short 'increase your fitness' promotional advertisement which they can record on tape – or they could make a video if you have the facilities.

Follow-up activity
The children may enjoy keeping an exercise log where they record the details of their activities. For example, they might write, 'Monday 17th May. Played rounders at school this afternoon. I didn't get that much exercise because I was on fourth post. Went swimming with Mum after school and did 10 lengths of the big pool.'

1 hour Have you joined in and joined up?

What you need and preparation
A few days before you plan to do this activity, collect some leaflets, application forms, posters and so on from a local leisure centre. Ask the children to bring in any examples of this kind of promotional literature they may have at home. Make a photocopy of the application forms. You will also need an enlarged map of the local area, brochures, catalogues or magazines selling sports equipment and a local directory or Yellow Pages.

What to do
15 mins Introduction
Begin by asking the children what kind of clubs are there that they could join – swimming clubs, riding schools, mountain bike clubs, gymnasiums and after school clubs and so on. Do any of the children in the class belong to a sports club or a leisure centre? What sort of clubs do they belong to? How often do they attend these clubs and leisure centres? How did they find out about them in the first place? What did they have to do to join?

Discuss the sort of promotional and membership literature you have collected. What kind of information is given in material of this kind? Talk about how an application form works – what sorts of information do they ask you? Explain to the children that they are going to find out how to join a club.

30 mins Development
Divide the class into small groups and give each group a task as follows:
● *Group 1* Using a copy of the local telephone directory, find out where various sports and leisure facilities are located. These can be plotted on an enlarged map of the vicinity.
● *Group 2* This group should write a 'how to join' advice card for somebody new to the school

Learning objectives
● Learn how to join a club as part of learning about managing exercise and fitness levels.

Lesson organisation
Initial, whole-class discussion; small group work; plenary.

Vocabulary
leisure
application
membership
advertising

who is interested in joining one of the after school sports clubs. The information should include, for example, the name of the club, when and where it takes place, any special equipment needed and the name of the adult in charge.

● *Group 3* Using the literature from the local clubs, or from their own knowledge of a particular club, design an advertising poster. This should include the name and location of the club, who it caters for, the sort of facilities it offers its members and contact addresses.

● *Group 4* Using the photocopies of the application forms, practise filling them in. They can they try to design a simple one of their own for a club they know about – or would like to start.

● *Group 5* Using the catalogues and magazines, the children investigate how much it would cost to join a tennis (or any other sport) club if they have never played before. The calculations should include the membership fee if there is one, the cost of clothing and equipment and any transport costs.

(15 mins) Plenary

Gather the class together to discuss the findings of each group. Which local sports facilities are the closest or the furthest away from the school? What sorts of costs are involved in joining a club? Remind the children that they must always talk to their parents/carers before making any decisions about joining a club.

Differentiation

As well as introducing the children to the processes involved in joining a club, the group tasks provide opportunities for reinforcement in a range of subjects – maths, geography, ICT and literacy. The children can therefore be allocated to groups according to their strengths or their need for extra work in one of these subject areas.

Assessing learning outcomes

How well do the children understand the processes involved in joining a club? Do they, for example, understand the financial or logistical implications? Do the children understand why it is necessary for clubs and leisure centres to advertise?

ICT opportunities
The children could use the software available to design a poster, format an application form or write and illustrate advice on how to join a club. The children could also send an e-mail or fax to a local club asking for additional information.

1 hour Can exercise hurt you?

What you need and preparation

Gather together reference materials on muscles and joints. Organise for the children to have access to a computer with word-processing software. You will also need copies of photocopiable page 117.

What to do

15 mins Introduction

The aim of this activity is to alert children to the potential dangers of exercising incorrectly or at the wrong times such as immediately after eating or when they are feeling unwell.

Remind the children that in PE and games lessons, they are always asked to warm up first. Can the children remember the sorts of things they are asked to do during these warm-up sessions? What sorts of movements are they asked to practise (stretching arms and legs, bending and straightening, walking briskly, jogging, skipping and so on)? Can they tell you why they are asked to warm up – what does this actually mean? Can they recall seeing professional sportsmen and women doing similar kinds of movements before they begin playing?

If you have room in the classroom you could ask the children to demonstrate one or two stretching and bending movements. Ask them to pinpoint which parts of their bodies are actually being warmed up. For example, can they feel their leg muscles being gently stretched and tightened and their backs straightening and bending? Ask the children to discuss why warming up these different muscle groups is important – what might happen if we don't do this? Can any of them recall and relate experiences they've had when they have pulled muscles or got a 'stitch' during or after exercise?

Talk to the children about the importance of exercising at the right times – for example it's not a good idea to do vigorous exercise directly after a big meal or when recovering from an illness as this can put excessive strain on the body.

Explain to the children that they are going to produce a class chart about the dos and don'ts of exercise.

35 mins Development

Give each child, or pair of children, photocopiable page 117 and ask them to list as many dos and don'ts in the appropriate column as they can think of. Explain that their lists could include short explanations, for example 'always warm up first otherwise you could pull a muscle' or 'never exercise straight after a meal or you could get stomach cramps'.

Get the children to cut out the phrases in the boxes on the sheet and place them in the correct column. With a partner they could play a game of 'odd-one-out' by taking turns to

Keeping fit

ICT opportunities

• The children can use a computer to present their ideas lists. The sheets containing their ideas can be divided into two sets – dos and don'ts – and the children can take turns to type them into the computer, print them out and illustrate them with their own hand-drawn diagrams, pictures cut out from magazines or downloaded from the Internet.

• If you have access to the Internet the children could also find further information about exercise and safety procedures from organisations such as Sport England, or the Health Education Council.

Follow-up activity

The children could go on to produce a more in-depth piece of work about exercise, muscle groups and safety procedures. This could be in the form of an information pack or illustrated booklet for others to use.

deliberately place a phrase in the wrong column – for example 'always eat a big, greasy meal before sport' in the 'always' column. When they've had a few turns each at this ask the children to make up some more words or phrases to add to the two lists and play the odd-one-out game again. Their new words could focus on aspects of sport and physical activity such as sporting injury, sport and hygiene or sport and disability.

A final version of the golden rules for staying injury free in sport could be made into a poster to display in the school hall or gym.

(10 mins) Plenary

Discuss the children's outcomes with the whole class and recap on the importance of exercising correctly and at the right times. Talk about how these ideas can be collated and made into a poster or chart for others to share. Where would be a good place to display this poster or chart – perhaps in the hall or on a board in the main corridor?

Differentiation

Younger or less able children could make their dos and don'ts lists more pictorial and keep their explanations shorter.

Older and more able children could carry out further research into the sorts of problems that can arise from over use of certain muscle groups (such as tennis elbow or knee problems in footballers). They could also produce labelled diagrams showing what actually happens to muscles as they stretch and contract.

Assessing learning outcomes

Can the children demonstrate through discussion and their sheets that they understand the importance of warming up before exercise and of exercising at the right times? Do the children understand the sorts of problems that can occur if they overuse certain muscles?

What happens to your body when you exercise?

(1 hour)

What you need and preparation

You will need stopwatches or timers, reference materials on the human body and three or four balloons. If possible organise for the class to take place in the hall. You will also need writing materials.

What to do

Introduction
(15 mins)

Explain to the class that they are going to find out what actually happens to our bodies during exercise. Talk about what muscles and joints are and help the children to locate these on their own bodies, or on a skeleton if you have one in school. Explain the difference between a ball and socket joint (shoulder) and a hinge joint (knee, ankle). Ask the children to move their shoulders around and compare this movement with the ankle and knee joints. Talk about how we use these joints when we move and exercise. Ask the children to tell you where in their bodies their hearts and lungs are and discuss what these organs do. Help the children to locate their pulse. (If they find it difficult to find the pulse point in their wrists, try asking them to find a pulse point in their neck.)

Development
(35 mins)

Divide the class into three groups and ask each group to find a space to work in. They will need writing materials with them to record the results of their investigations. Give each group a task as follows. (If there is enough time the children could have a go at more than one of the group activities.)

● *Group 1:* the heart group
The children should take their pulses while they are sitting or standing still and record them. Next they should run on the spot as fast as they can for three minutes and record their pulse rates again. They can then compare the differences between the two readings. Their task then is to find out from reference books what happens to the heart and blood flow during exercise. The main point as far as exercise is concerned is that the heart is a very large muscle and if it is to remain healthy it must, as with all other muscles, be exercised regularly.

● *Group 2:* the muscles group
The children should concentrate on the muscles in arms and legs. First the children write a few words to describe how their arms and legs feel when they are sitting or standing still. They will generally come up with words such as *light, relaxed, normal* and so on. The children should then skip on the spot (or use skipping ropes) for three minutes. Alternatively they can lift their arms from waist to shoulder height continuously for three minutes. They then write a few words to describe how their arms and legs feel now (*tired, achy, wobbly, weak, heavy* and so on.) This group should then research which arm and legs muscles are involved in these movements and how they work together.

● *Group 3:* the lungs group

This group is given a balloon each and should record how many puffs it takes them to inflate it. They should then run on the spot, hop or jump for three minutes. They then try inflating the balloon again, recording how many puffs it takes this time and comparing the difference. The research task for this group is to find out more about the lungs and the flow of oxygen necessary to keep them healthy.

10 mins **Plenary**

Ask each group to report back on its findings. What differences have they noticed about 'at rest' pulse rates, muscles and lungs and after exercise? What have they found out about how these different muscles and organs work? What can the children deduce about the importance of exercise for these parts of the body? Can they explain how their muscles feel before and after exercise?

Differentiation

Younger or less able children can concentrate on the practical aspects of the exercise, rather than on the further research. For these children it may be easier for them to work in pairs. One child can then take the other's pulse, time the exercise and record the results. These children can then be asked to write a short account (in words and pictures) of their experiment.

Older or more able children can more easily manage the timings and recording themselves. Some children can carry out quite in-depth research into aspects of health such as the effect of smoking on the heart and lungs.

Assessing learning outcomes

Can the children locate their heart, pulse, lungs, arm and leg muscles on their own bodies? Do the children understand that during and after exercise the pulse rate increases and we need to breathe more rapidly to take the extra oxygen we need into our lungs as we exercise? Do they understand that our muscles feel different before and after exercise? Can older or more able children find out the effects of smoking on our heart and lungs?

ICT opportunities
Ask the children to collect the results of the different groups investigations and record them on a simple database.

Can you invent your own games?

1 hour

What you need and preparation

Gather together photographs or magazine pictures of disabled sportsmen and women, for example those participating in the Paralympics or the London marathon. You will also need copies of photocopiable pages 118 and 119 and writing materials. If possible, organise for the plenary to be held in a large area.

What to do

Introduction
10 mins

Explain to the children that they are going to invent a brand new game to encourage other people to exercise more. Talk about the sorts of games they already play – which are their favourites? Discuss the different sorts of games that are played in different seasons. Do the children think it is easier to exercise in the summer or the winter? Next ask the children to consider how people who are disabled can manage the exercise they also need. How can people in wheelchairs for example try to ensure that they exercise their strongest muscles and joints to stay as strong and fit as possible? Share and discuss some of the photographs you have collected.

Tell the children that the class will be divided into three sets: one will be inventing a new game to play in the winter; one will look at a new summer game, and the third group will be working on a new game for people whose movements are limited through disability.

Development
40 mins

Give each group the appropriate photocopiable page and make sure they understand what is required of them. Talk about the sorts of equipment they are allowed to use in their new game.

The children then work out as a group how to invent a new game using the equipment, venues and seasons given on the sheet. Each group should come up with a name for their new game, describe the rules and how it works, how a goal or point is scored, explain who would benefit from or enjoy it most, why it's particularly beneficial for muscle growth, hand-eye co-ordination and a healthy body and so on. They can record any extra explanations on the back of the sheets.

Plenary
10 mins

Ask each group to explain their game and invite others to offer further suggestions for refinements and modifications. If you have access to a large space, the children can try out their games. They can then make further refinements and changes as necessary.

Learning objectives
• Invent high exercise games to encourage others to take more exercise.
• Compare the sorts of games it is possible to play in different seasons.
• Understand the exercise needs of disabled people.

Lesson organisation
Initial teacher-led introduction; individual or small group activity; plenary.

Vocabulary
equipment
seasonal games
disability
rules

Keeping fit

Differentiation

Younger or less able children may find it easier to invent such games through practical trial and error. They will almost certainly find it easier to invent a game if given fewer pieces of equipment. The game for disabled people therefore may be an especially good starting point for them. Let these children experiment with the equipment and encourage them to keep the rules simple. They may also need extra support – perhaps during the Literacy Hour – to record the rules and benefits of their games. Alternatively they could speak the rules into a tape recorder.

Older and more able children can generally formulate their games on paper first. Their explanations concerning the merits of the game can be based on further research into how the muscles and joints work.

ICT opportunities
• The children's inventions can be listed on a simple database showing the name of the game, number of players, equipment needed and so on. Alternatively, the children can write a rules sheet for their game and print it out ready for people to play.
• They could also design and produce a poster or leaflet for their new game using a word processor and art program.

Follow-up activity
The children could invite other classes to try out their new games. If appropriate you could invite a disabled member of the community to visit the school and try out the games designed specifically for them.

Assessing learning outcomes

Do the children appreciate the differences between the sorts of games and exercise that are possible in different seasons? Can the children use simple pieces of equipment to invent a game, which is especially beneficial for certain parts of the body or functions such as leg muscles, hand-eye co-ordination or balance?

Building healthy environments

Building a healthy environment and ensuring that there will be adequate resources for future generations is clearly vital to the continued existence of the human race. Yet the impact that man had in the last century alone on the global environment is well documented. There is a hole in the Ozone layer linked to an increasing number of skin cancer sufferers, while flooding in both the Northern and Southern hemispheres is becoming an almost commonplace occurrence.

Rainforests – which act like huge lungs, filtering out the harmful atmospheric elements – are being destroyed at a rate of about 50 million hectares per year, and the effects of deforestation are beginning to be felt across the globe.

As this chapter is about the environment, the activities provide several opportunities for outside visits. These are not expensive suggestions – most of them require you to do no more than go for a walk around the vacinity of the school, although it is recommended that a trip to a local recycling centre should be arranged if possible.

Environmental issues have been somewhat edged out of the National Curriculum in recent years, largely to make way for the literacy and numeracy strategies. And yet children are often passionately interested in environmental projects on endangered species, conservation, alternative technology, pollution and recycling. Indeed it has often been said that children seem to care more about 'green' issues than their parents.

This chapter focuses on the key environmental issues of resource and waste management and the concept of global responsibility. These two broad areas encompass the main current concerns about the health – or otherwise – of the planet on which we live. Through the activities the children are asked to consider how waste is generated, the effects of excessive packaging, the importance of energy and resource conservation and the detrimental effects of waste on the environment if we fail to manage it properly.

The second unit is designed to reinforce the 'think global – act local' message. The thinking behind this message is that if we all try to make an effort to improve and sustain a healthy environment then collectively we may be able to halt the present global levels of damage. Children are asked to make observations about their own local environment, beginning – literally – in their own backyard, or at least, the school grounds. The activities go on to suggest some outside work around the local community, investigating hedgerows, and also bring in the idea of charity as a way to share resources globally.

Because 'environmental education' has become something of a marginalised subject it is important to find alternative ways of integrating key environmental issues into other subject areas. There are many opportunities in the activities for the children to practise their literacy and numeracy skills and to make effective use of Information and communication technology. There are also opportunities for linking the activities in this chapter with the geography curriculum and schemes of work.

Waste not want not

The activities in this unit focus on the following environmental themes:
● waste as an inevitable part of all processes and the impact waste products have on the environment
● recycling
● packaging
● water conservation
● pollution.

These are familiar themes and the children are likely to know something about all of them. In fact it is often said that children are more environmentally aware than adults, so it makes sense to build on what they know. For this reason the activities use ordinary, everyday objects such as packaging as a stimulus for discussion.

There are many children's books that deal with the theme of waste – *Stig of the Dump* and *The Iron Man* being among the most famous. Stories make excellent launch pads for considering the impact waste has on the environment.

Through the activities on waste and recycling children learn that waste is inevitable and that the problem is in the control and management of it. Basically the more we produce the more we have to dispose of. The work on packaging aims to encourage the children to reflect on what packaging is actually for and how much of it is strictly necessary. The aim is to help children to become environmentally conscious consumers in the long term.

The activity suggestions in this unit will also reinforce learning in other key curriculum areas, notably science and literacy.

UNIT: Waste not want not

Enquiry questions	Learning objectives	Teaching activities	Learning outcomes	Cross-curricular links
What is waste?	• Learn about waste as an environmental issue. • Identify how waste is created from everyday activities.	Share fiction about waste and the environment. Work from a photocopiable sheet and draw conclusions. Collation of ideas into a class frieze.	*Children:* • identify how waste is created • explain why managing waste is a serious environmental issue	Science: living things. English: shared reading. Art: working with mixed media.
Can you use that again?	• Learn about recycling waste products. • Identify which waste products can be successfully recycled.	Introduction to the theme of recycling waste. Class visit to a local recycling centre. Follow-up work.	• explain what recycling is and why it is important • describe the process of recycling	Science: materials and their properties.
What's under wraps?	• Focus attention on packaging as an environmental issue. • Learn that some packaging is essential and some is wasteful. • Identify properties of materials. • Match packaging to purpose.	Introductory class discussion through a collection of packaging. Decide which packaging is appropriate through sorting and classifying.	• recognise when a product has been over-packaged • identify which sorts of packaging are environmentally harmful	Science: materials and their properties; classification.
Are we awash with water?	• Understand the central importance of water in our lives. • Consider how water can be conserved. • Devise strategies for saving water.	Discussion about water in the environment. Class work on the water cycle. Follow-up work on water conservation.	• describe the water cycle • suggest practical ways of saving water	Geography: the water cycle; the Earth's resources. Science: living things.
What is pollution?	• Learn about the causes and effects of pollution.	Discussion through pictorial evidence. Work with photocopiable sheet.	• identify types of pollution • suggest ways of avoiding pollution.	Science: waste; living things. Geography: the environment.

Resources
Children's literature on the theme of waste/pollution, a collection of different types of packaging, photographs showing wetlands, deserts, floods and so on, pictures showing environmental disasters.

Display
Photographs of man-made environmental disasters.

Waste not
want not

1 hour What is waste?

Learning objectives
• Learn about waste as an environmental issue.
• Identify and consider how waste is created from everyday processes and activities.

Lesson organisation
Teacher-led, whole-class discussion; individual follow-up work; plenary.

Vocabulary
waste
by-product
materials
processes
pollution
sewage
litter
rubbish

What you need and preparation

Gather together some children's literature on the theme of waste. There are many examples of the genre and the class or school library is almost certain to contain some or all of the following popular titles:

● *Stig of the Dump*, by Clive King (Puffin Books)
● *Professor Noah's Spaceship*, by Brian Wildsmith (OUP)
● *Charlie's House*, by Reviva Schermbrucker (Walker)
● *The Iron Man*, by Ted Hughes (Faber Children's Books).

Clearly you will choose the ones appropriate to the age of the children but this is not strictly necessary. It is sometimes useful to read a picture book written for a younger audience with the children as this helps them to focus their attention on the messages being explored in the story.

You will also need a large piece of paper displayed on the wall and copies of photocopiable page 120.

What to do

20 mins Introduction

Introduce the class to the theme of waste and share some of the suggested stories with them. Encourage the children to discuss how waste materials feature in the stories. What are the main messages? Work with the children to decide on a definition of waste, for example 'the materials and substances that are left over when products are made and which have to be disposed of'. Write your agreed definition on a large piece of paper.

Ask the children to name as many things as they can think of that can be regarded as waste. Remind them about waste water and sewage and so on. List their contributions on the board or a flip chart for the children to refer to later.

30 mins Development

Give each child a copy of photocopiable page 120. This asks the children to think about and identify the waste products that are created by three different processes – eating, travelling around and staying warm. Ask the children to talk about any of the words they don't know and work through one example with the whole class. The children then match the 'waste words' to the illustrations and write a sentence about one of the words.

On a separate piece of paper ask the children to show in pictures or words how they think one aspect of waste is managed – what do they know for example about what happens to the content of our dustbins or where water goes when you pour it down the sink? Can they show how a waste product such as a yoghurt pot or plastic bottle can be recycled into a seed pot or pencil pot for example?

10 mins **Plenary**
Discuss the children's outcomes and invite them to add any other waste-producing processes they have thought of. Recap on the idea that all processes involve a waste product and these waste products can pose a significant threat to the environment if they are not managed properly.

Differentiation
Older and more able children can go on to research more into waste products, how they are managed and their impact on the environment. The children can also make their own versions of the worksheet by using different picture clues.

Assessing learning outcomes
Do the children understand that all processes create waste? Can the children identify the waste products created from common place activities and products? Do the children recognise the impact waste products can have on the environment and understand the need to minimise the creation of waste?

4 hours # Can you use that again?

What you need and preparation
Access to a local recycling centre. A couple of weeks before you plan to take the children on the visit to your nearest recycling centre, contact the local council to make all the necessary arrangements, discussing with them the sorts of things the children will be able to see such as can crushing, newspaper recycling and so on.

You will also need adult helpers, preferably parents or carers to accompany you when you take the class to the site, a camera and writing materials.

What to do
30 mins **Introduction**
Before you take the children to the recycling centre recap on what we actually mean by recycling (reusing materials that would otherwise be wasted). Ask the children to tell you the sorts of materials that are commonly recycled such as paper, aluminium and cans, glass, clothing, corks and so on. Why is recycling an important aspect of building and sustaining a healthy environment? Explain to the children that they are going to find out what happens to the cans, paper, glass and so on after it is put into the big recycling bins they will have seen in their local environment, or the school grounds.

Tell the children that later they are going to make a class book about the recycling centre.

3 hours **20** mins **Development**
With your adult volunteers take the children on the visit to the local recycling centre. Explain to the children that at the centre they should watch the processes carefully and ask questions. They are not expected to take notes at this stage or fill in any worksheets.

If the children have brought a camera with them, encourage them to take photographs of the different activities they will see during the visit. It is also important that you or another of the adult helpers takes photographs of the whole visit as you will need these later to illustrate the book you will be making.

Back in the classroom, discuss the children's main observations and allow them plenty of

time to ask questions and describe what they found particularly interesting or surprising. Ask the children to think of some adjectives to describe the machinery and containers they saw, the sounds they heard and their thoughts. Write their describing words on the board or a flip chart. These can later be included in the class recycling book.

Discuss with the children what the class book could contain, how they could all make a contribution and how they can make it interesting and enjoyable for others to read.

You may decide to divide the class into writing, design and production teams. The design team could concentrate on the look and format of the book, the writing team could provide the text and the production team could collate the materials, work out deadlines and take responsibility for putting the book together. Alternatively groups of children could work on different aspects of the visit and the processes they observed. For example, one group could work on the story of what the class actually did and in what order, another group could focus on particular aspects of the recycling process and another group could focus on the benefits of recycling waste.

Plenary
10 mins When the class book is complete and the class has suggested a title, another class perhaps of younger children could be invited in during the Literacy Hour to share the book.

Differentiation
The variety of tasks involved in the making of a book on recycling lends itself to the needs and interests of different individuals within the class. Let the children work on those aspects of the process that appeal most to them and which allow them to reinforce their strengths – for example in art and design or writing.

More able or older children can go on to investigate the pros and cons of recycling certain materials, for example the costs involved in using cullet in the glass-making process as compared to using raw materials alone.

Assessing learning outcomes
Can the children show that they understand the environmental significance of recycling? Can the children describe the journey of a recycled carton or can?

1 hour What's under wraps?

What you need and preparation

A collection of different kinds of packaging, including food packets and wrappers, drinks cartons, the wrappings used for selling clothes, office equipment and luxury items such as cosmetics.

A few days before you plan to begin this activity ask the children to bring this kind of packaging in from home. You will also need photocopiable page 121.

What to do

20 mins Introduction

Explain to the children that you would like them to think about packaging. What do they understand by the word *packaging* – what examples can they think of? Talk about all the different sorts of packaging in your stimulus collection and ask the children why they think it has been used. Is it all necessary? Why do we need it?

In order for the children to get a balanced view on the significance of packaging as an environmental issue they need to understand that packaging is both a good and a bad thing. The main purposes of packaging are to enable products to be transported more easily and to stop food from going bad. Explain to the children that

two things make food go bad: bacteria and other micro-organisms, which can get into food, and natural chemicals in food called enzymes, which cause it to go bad.

It is often with luxury goods such as cosmetics that we find excess packaging – used to make the product more appealing to the customer. With the children, look at the collection of packaging and make comparisons about the amount of packaging used for different products. Comparing an empty milk or juice carton with a print cartridge for the computer is a good place to begin.

However, packaging threatens the health of the environment if it is used excessively. Ask the children how much of the packaging in your collection is unnecessary – a folded shirt in cellophane wrapping is a good example.

30 mins Development

Ask the children to find different ways of sorting and classifying waste packaging, for example, by the type of material from which it is made, the purposes it serves (storing food, transporting items from the shops and so on) or whether it can be recycled. Before they begin, make sure the children understand what we mean by recycling – try writing a definition.

Now give each child a copy of photocopiable page 121 and help them to make their classifications.

10 mins Plenary

Discuss the results of the children's charts from the photocopiable page and ask them for their ideas from the rest of the sheet. Can they see when a product has been over-packaged?

Learning objectives
• Focus attention on packaging and its significance for a healthy environment.
• Understand that some packaging is essential and some is unnecessary and wasteful of resources.
• Identify the environmentally significant properties of certain materials.
• Identify which packaging is best suited to different purposes and to understand of the impact of waste on the environment.

Lesson organisation
Initial teacher-led discussion followed by individual work; plenary.

Vocabulary
packaging
wrappings
cartons
containers
reusable
energy
crush
flattened
enzymes
micro-organisms

Waste not
want not

Which packaging is safest for the environment? Talk about how they will use this information. Will they now choose products with less packaging? Will they choose products with recyclable packaging?

Differentiation

Less able or younger children will find it helpful to physically sort the packaging from the stimulus collection. They can be given hoops or circular pieces of card into which to place their groups of different sorts of packaging. Some may be able to produce Venn diagrams from these sets.

Older and more able children can try devising another table similar to the one shown on the photocopiable sheet. Encourage them to use new headings such as 'Is it made from a renewable resource?' or 'Is it expensive to produce?'

Assessing learning outcomes

Can the children show that they recognise when a product has been over-packaged? Can the children classify packaging into sets reflecting their implications for a healthy environment?

ICT opportunities
The children could send an e-mail a local company asking them for information on their packaging and recycling practices. Alternatively they could send a fax or ring them up.

① Are we awash with water?
hour

Learning objectives
• Recognise the central importance of water in our daily lives.
• Understand that water is a precious, sometimes scarce, natural resource which needs to be managed properly and conserved.
• Suggest strategies for conserving water.

Lesson organisation
Initial teacher-led class discussion; individual follow-up work; children then work in pairs to reinforce the issues; plenary.

What you need and preparation

Gather together photographs or pictures from magazines showing wetlands, deserts, flooded villages and so on. You will also need photcopiable pages 122 and 123.

What to do

15 mins Introduction

Share the pictures of flooded and parched landscapes with the children as a way of introducing them to the central importance of water in everyone's lives. Establish that they understand that water is essential for all forms of life – animal, plant and human. Ask the children to tell you all the different times of the day they use water and for what purpose – making drinks, washing, cooking, flushing the toilet, cleaning their teeth and so on. List these on the board or flip chart.

Explain to the children that the energy costs of getting water into our taps in a condition that is safe and clean to use are very high, and that we all need to be careful not to waste water.

40 mins Development

Using photocopiable page 122, explain and discuss the water cycle to the whole class and give the children opportunities to ask questions. Ask each child to fill in the missing words and labels on the sheet so that they are all familiar with where water comes from on its journey to our taps. Don't spend

too long on this aspect of the activity – 10–15 minutes should be adequate.

Ask the class to brainstorm all the ways they can think of to save water (have a shower rather than a bath if possible, flush the toilet only when necessary, don't overfill kettles or leave taps running and so on). How many of these do the children already do regularly? Do other members of the school and home community also do these things?

Hand out the copies of photocopiable page 123 and ask the children to write a sentence under each picture about how they can save water in that area. Ask the children to work in pairs to make a 'Saving Water the Easy Way' card for a local water company to send out to their customers. They can work with the ideas introduced on photocopiable page 123 – and go on to add other ideas of their own.

Vocabulary
water conservation
the water cycle
aquatic life
clouds
river
lake
estuary
sea
evaporates
condenses
rain
ground

(5 mins) Plenary
Call the children back together and discuss their ideas for saving water and their plans for the 'Saving Water the Easy Way' card. Do they think it would be a good idea to display a card like this in the cloakrooms to remind other children to save water?

Differentiation

Younger and less able children can concentrate on illustrating one or two ideas for saving water while the older or more able children can develop three or four ideas. Make sure the children are all familiar with the vocabulary and help them to use these words in their cards.

Some children will be able to write to your local water company asking for information about the water cycle and their attempts to make the management of their water supply more efficient and environmentally friendly.

ICT opportunities
• The children can use the Internet or CD-ROMs to research areas of the world that are desperately short of water. They can find out how this affects the daily lives of the people who live there – how far for example do some African women and children have to walk to collect their water from the nearest well or river?
• The children can also telephone, fax or e-mail your local water company to ask if it would be possible to visit their treatment works.

Follow-up activity
Take the children on a visit to the local water treatment works to let them experience for themselves the processes involved in collecting, treating and distributing water.

Assessing learning outcomes

Do the children understand the different stages in the water cycle? Can the children suggest ways of saving water in school and at home?

CHAPTER 3
BUILDING HEALTHY ENVIRONMENTS

**Waste not
want not**

① What is pollution?

Learning objectives
• Learn about the environmental issues relating to various forms of pollution.
• Understand that all processes involve a waste product and that careless management of these waste products poses a serious threat to the environment.

Lesson organisation
Initial teacher-led discussion; individual follow-up work; plenary.

Vocabulary
pollution
waste management
poisons
toxins
environment

What you need and preparation
Gather together some pictures of environmental disasters such as the Exxon Valdez oil spill, rivers contaminated by industrial and agricultural chemicals, pesticides and fertilisers, atomic mushroom clouds and the Chernobyl atomic catastrophe. You will also need photcopiable page 124.

What to do

15 mins **Introduction**
Introduce the subject of pollution by showing the class the pictures of environmental disasters and talk about the effects these had on marine, animal, plant and human life. Ask the children to tell you about all the different forms of pollution they have heard of such as litter, oil slicks, acid rain, chemical spillages, car exhaust and so on. Can the children name any potential sources of pollution such as industrial chimneys, oil refineries, chemical or packaging companies, agricultural waste accidentally getting into the water supply, the fall out from refineries and so on?

Remind them that there is also something called noise pollution and ask them to consider what sorts of things cause uncomfortable levels of noise. Examples could include traffic noise, noise from quarrying activities and machinery, loud music and so on.

30 mins **Development**
Give each child a copy of photocopiable page 124 and explain to them that they need to fill in three examples of each type of pollution. Ask the class for their initial ideas under each section before they attempt to complete the rest of the sheet.

Collect the sheets in and cut them into three so that you have a set of ideas for each heading. These can then be made into a wall display and can be used as the basis for more detailed individual drawings and explanations of different types of pollution.

Alternatively, the children could work in three groups to produce a large wall frieze of the main types of pollution to display in the classroom or school hall. For example, one group could produce a collage from recycled materials showing how household waste is created, while another could depict what happens to car exhaust fumes and the effect they have on the ozone layer. Ask the children to add a few phrases to their collages and drawings suggesting some practical ways of reducing pollution such as using their bicycles rather than the family car, or more recycling banks in their local community.

15 mins **Plenary**
Discuss the wall display with the class. Can they think of any other forms and sources of pollution?

Ask the children how they can help to reduce levels of pollution in their local environment. These ideas could include making sure they don't drop litter at school or outside, talking to their parents or carers about more efficient waste disposal, lobbying local MPs to put pressure on local companies to reduce their levels of pollution, writing to these local companies to express their concern or writing articles to raise the issues with the local media and so on. Teach the children the 'think global – act local' conservation message.

Differentiation
Younger and less able children will generally find it easier to focus on just one form of pollution such as noise or litter. They can make a scrapbook of cuttings showing pictures of environmental pollution with simple labels and captions.

Older or more able children can actually write letters to MPs and local councillors asking them to take up the issue of local pollution. They can also write articles for newspapers or school newspapers to alert parents and the local community to the dangers of pollution and suggesting some ways of tackling the problem.

Assessing learning outcomes
Are the children able to explain what pollution is, what forms it can take and explain the impact on the environment? Can the children offer practical suggestions for reducing levels of pollution both locally and globally?

Think global – act local

The aim of this unit is to encourage the children to take an active part in building a healthy environment. The idea of 'Think global – act local' is that the process of building a healthy environment can begin, literally, in one's own backyard. Our immediate environments – the school and local community – are in a sense microcosms of the global picture. Taking steps to improve our own immediate environment contributes to the health of the world as a whole. The children need to know that what they do and how they act really can make a difference. The environmental themes considered in this unit are:

● **gardens and their place in healthy environments**

Creating a garden from a neglected piece of ground is one of the best ways of teaching children about healthy environments. It also reinforces learning in almost all other areas of the curriculum, notably science, numeracy and geography. You don't have to be Alan Titchmarsh to work with the children on creating a garden. Nor do you need access to a huge plot. The children can learn much from growing plants in pots or even planting up and maintaining a window box. For the more ambitious or green-fingered, extending the project to include a complete make over for the school grounds can be hugely rewarding. Schools that have created wildlife gardens, ponds, quiet areas and so on have found that it brings in parents and local businesses and engages the children in active learning about the environment.

● **improving the look and environmental well-being of the school**

The activity 'Can we make it happen?' further encourages the children to be active in their improvement of the environment. It offers the children the opportunity to reflect on the aesthetics of their school environment and suggests ways of putting their recommendations into practice.

● **wildlife, habitats and endangered species**

Understanding the environmental importance of wildlife, nature habitats and endangered species is an essential part of building healthy environments and here the children are encouraged to study, observe and comment on local issues relating to this environmental theme. They are asked to form an opinion on whether they think zoos and wildlife centres are a good or bad thing in terms of conservation and also to act as environmental detectives in their own locality. There are opportunities in this unit for the children to investigate hedgerows and to identify threats to local wildlife habitats posed by 'artificial' fences.

● **hedgerows and the local environment**

This unit also looks at the importance of local wildlife and flora and fauna. A visit to a zoo or wildlife park is recommended as a stimulus for learning about endangered species and the loss of local and global habitats.

● **charity and support for environmental issues**

The final activity in this unit extends the concept of 'Think global – act local' to encompass the role of charities in safeguarding the local and international environment and encourages children to make informed, democratic decisions.

UNIT: Think global – act local

Enquiry questions	Learning objectives	Teaching activities	Learning outcomes	Cross-curricular links
What's in a gardener's world?	• Turn a piece of neglected land into an environmentally sustainable garden. • Learn the benefits of gardens to the well-being of the school environment and the individuals within it. • Work with plants and soil in order to understand how things grow and how important this is for a healthy environment.	Initial discussion explaining the garden project. Undertake tasks and planning with the aim of starting a garden in the school grounds.	*Children:* • can identify the tasks involved in creating a garden • describe why gardens are important to the environment	Geography: making judgements about the school environment. Science: living things.
Can we make it happen?	• Improve the look and feel of the school as an environment. • Learn about lobbying for change through reasoned debate.	Short walk around the school. Work in groups to suggest improvements and decide how to make progress with ideas.	• identify areas for improvement • understand that making positive suggestions is part of citizenship	English: writing letters. ICT: sending e-mails/faxes.
What do we know about wildlife?	• Reflect on why we have zoos and consider their environmental significance. • Investigate the global significance of endangered species.	Introduction to the topic of zoos and wildlife. Class visit to nearest wildlife venue. Follow-up work from the visit, beginning with a photocopiable sheet.	• explain the role of zoos in preserving species • express views on the advantages and disadvantages of zoos	Science: living things. Geography: habitats; conservation.
What's on the other side of the hedge?	• Understand the environmental importance of hedgerows. • Understand the implications of habitat loss. • Identify hedgerow creatures.	Short walk around the vicinity. Count and record evidence of hedgerow life and dangers to natural habitats.	• understand that hedgerows contain important environmental balances • identify some threats to hedgerows	Science: living things. Geography: aesthetics and the environment.
Which charity?	• Understand how to help others through an established charity. • See how the democratic process works when collective decisions need to be made. • Become familiar with the works and aims of a range of charities.	Initial sharing of ideas with whole class. Small-group investigations.	• identify a range of charities and what they do • work collaboratively.	ICT: Internet research.

Resources
Gardening equipment, small plot of land or window boxes, camera, reference material on trees and hedgerows, clip boards, leaflets and so on related to environmental issues.

Display
Pictures of different types of gardens.

What's in a gardener's world?

Learning objectives
• Turn a neglected piece of ground into an environmentally sustainable garden.
• Learn the benefits of gardens to the well-being of the school environment and the individuals within it.
• Work with plants and soil in order to understand how things grow and how important this is for a healthy environment.

Classroom organisation
Initial whole-class discussion to share ideas; small-group and individual work; plenary.

Vocabulary
garden
herbs
flowers
sensory
growth
compost
soil
organic
donations

What you need and preparation

Ideally you will have access to a small piece of ground that isn't being used for anything else somewhere in the school grounds. It doesn't have to be large – it is perfectly possible for children to understand the environmental messages and get great enjoyment from a few metres of neglected soil, a paved area where you plants can be grown in pots or even a window box. You will also need a selection of gardening tools including trowels, forks and gloves. Gather together pictures of different kinds of gardens from magazines.

You may also be able to prepare for this lesson by taking the class on a visit to a local garden centre, park or stately home to get some ideas for the type of garden you would like to create.

If you are particularly enthusiastic and have the space, this activity can be developed into a whole school project involving parents and carers and volunteers from the local community.

What to do

Introduction
30 mins
Tell the children that you have been thinking about how the school grounds could be made more attractive by designing a garden. Show the children the pictures you have collected of different sorts of gardens and ask them which ones they like best. These could include herb gardens, vegetable gardens, sensory gardens, flower gardens and so on. Take the children to the site (even if this is to look at the amount of room you have on window ledges or paved areas around the school) and discuss what sort of garden they would like to create.

Development
50 mins
Discuss with the whole class the sort of jobs that will need to be done and make a list. These jobs will include clearing the ground of weeds, digging, composting, planting and general maintenance. Decide the order of these jobs and when they could be carried out. Decide together how you will raise any money needed for plants and equipment. If there are local garden centres near your school, you can approach the manager and ask for his/her help – this may be in the form of advice or donations. Parents/carers who are keen gardeners may also like to be involved, perhaps by actually coming into school to help the children with their various tasks or by giving you cuttings and so on.

Tell the children that they are going to keep a garden log that will record what has to be done, by when and by whom. The children then write in the log at the end of each gardening session describing what they did, how the money was found for the plants and so on, their observations about the soil, weeds and so on and a note of what needs to be done next. Agree when work on your new garden will begin and make sure all the children have a task to perform.

(10 mins) Plenary

At the end of this initial session, check that everyone agrees on the sort of garden you will create and that everyone knows what their tasks will be: to ask parents/carers for help, to write letters to potential donors, to bring in some garden tools and so on. Ask the children to complete their first garden log entry. Agree when your next gardening session will be and what needs to be done first.

Differentiation

Clearly the sorts of tasks involved in creating a garden will depend to a large extend on the amount of space you have available, the kind of garden you want, as well as the amount of time you can devote to it and the ages of the children. Creating a sensory garden will reinforce aspects of the science curriculum for younger children. With a sensory garden plants are selected for the sounds they create (grasses); smell (fragrant plants like honeysuckle, Jasmine and so on) their appearance (brightly coloured shrubs and flowers such as marigolds, lobelia and so on) and for their taste (mainly herbs).

> **ICT opportunities**
> ● Instead of the children each keeping their own garden log, the class could take turns to write entries in the class log written on the computer. Some children will be able to formulate a table to record specific things such as dates plants were planted, how much they have grown, how much they have spent, who has made donations and so on.
> ● The children could also keep a photographic record of progress in the garden, or make a video if you have the equipment.
> ● Help the children to send faxes and emails to local companies asking for donations.

Older children can take on more of the responsibility for raising funds, asking local businesses for donations of compost, plants, pots, tools and money if necessary. This older age group may also be able to take on some gardening tasks during lunch breaks and after school.

More able children or those with a real enthusiasm for the garden project will be able to investigate such things as soil types, the ideal growing conditions for certain kinds of plants, when and how to prune, organic methods of composting and feeding.

Assessing learning outcomes

Do the children understand what needs to be done to a neglected piece of ground in order to turn it into a garden? Can the children say why gardens are an important aspect of environmental health and well being? Can the children work collaboratively in groups to achieve the tasks taking into account the needs, wishes and opinions of others?

Think global –
act local

Can we make it happen?

1 hour 30 mins

What you need and preparation
Writing materials.

What to do

Introduction
30 mins
Take the children for a walk around the school including the playground, playing field, sports hall and so on. Ask them as they walk around the school to think about how different areas could be made more attractive and environmentally friendly. Explain that they are going to launch a campaign to try to put their ideas into practice.

Development
50 mins
Back in the classroom, share and discuss the children's observations and ideas for improvements. Remind the children that they can include things like more litter bins and recycling banks, quiet areas, seating areas, gardens and plants, notices to remind everyone to conserve water and electricity, access for disabled people and visitors to the school and so on.

Which of these ideas do the children think will be easiest and most difficult to achieve and how will they go about making it happen? How for example, will they communicate their ideas to the rest of the school including teachers and governors? Who will need to give permission for these ideas to be put into place?

Divide the children into small 'task groups' to tackle different aspects of your direct action campaign as follows:
● *Group 1* Make a plan of the school, mapping where improvements could be made for example, the location of recycling banks, litter bins, seating areas, better facilities for people with special needs and so on.
● *Group 2* Write a letter to the headteacher outlining the ideas the class has had for environmental improvements.
● *Group 3* Write a letter to parents asking for help and support for the project.
● *Group 4* Send faxes and e-mails to local businesses and environmental organisations asking for help, support and donations.

Plenary
10 mins
Bring the class back together and discuss the campaign strategy so far and any other ideas that have occurred to the children as they've been working on their letters and plans. Explain to the children that this sort of campaign is part of the democratic process, and that within a democracy everyone is entitled to an opinion and to take peaceful action in order to change things that need improving.

Think global –
act local

Differentiation

The activities for the different task groups outlined above will allow you to allocate children to the groups according to their needs and strengths. Younger and less able children will need help to draft their letters and you could perhaps make this part of the Literacy Hour.

Older and more able children can make an action plan recording what needs to be done, by whom and by when. They can then review this plan from time to time recording what has been achieved and how it came about. The children could submit this in the form of a report to the school council if you have one and/or the school governors.

Assessing learning outcomes

Can the children discuss how aesthetically and environmentally their immediate environment can be improved? Have the children understood that making suggestions for improvements to the appropriate people is part of the democratic process and an element of effective citizenship?

 ## What do we know about wildlife?

What you need and preparation

Access to a local zoo, wildlife park, wildfowl or bird sanctuary, or marina centre and so on. If a visit to one of these is not logistically feasible, this activity can be stimulated by pictures of animals and birds in captivity. A couple of weeks before you plan to take the children on the visit, contact the animal centre to make all the necessary arrangements, discussing with them the sorts of animals the children will be able to see. Make sure you have enough adult helpers to support you on the day. You will also need a camera and photocopiable page 125.

What to do

20 mins **Introduction**
Before taking the children to your chosen site, brainstorm all the different animals, birds fish and so on they are likely to see. What do the children already know about these creatures? What else would they like to find out? Discuss what we mean by endangered species – which animals and birds can the children name that are endangered? How do the children feel about animals and birds being kept in captivity? What reasons can the children think of for zoos, wildlife parks and so on?

4 hours **Development**
Take the children on the visit. Tell them that during the visit they can take notes if they want to, but that the most important thing is for them to make careful observations and ask questions.

Back in the classroom, ask the children who was able to find the answers to their questions? How easy was it to find the information they needed? If they still don't know the answers to their questions how else can they find out now?

Give the children a copy of photocopiable page 125 and ask them to fill it in. Explain to them that they should then use their sheets as a starting point for writing a short piece about their visit.

20 mins **Plenary**
Discuss with the children their answers to the questions on photocopiable page 125. What do they think are the advantages and disadvantages of zoos and so on are? What purpose for example do they serve for endangered species and the preservation of the global

---

Learning objectives
• Reflect on why we have zoos, wildlife parks and marina centres and so on and consider their environmental significance.
• Investigate the global significance of endangered species.

Lesson organisation
Initial class discussion; field trip; classroom follow-up; plenary.

Vocabulary
wildlife
captivity
conservation
endangered species
sanctuary

environment? How can the zoo or wildlife park play a part in the conservation of natural habitats?

Encourage them to think about how they can help to preserve these animals/birds and their natural habitats – perhaps by joining a wildlife or animal protection charity, looking after their own local environments in order to protect delicate ecosystems and so on.

Differentiation

Younger and less able children will enjoy finding out more about their favourite animal. They could collect pictures, amazing facts, information about their natural habitat and present the information as a set of picture cards.

Older and more able children can investigate the causes of loss of habitats (ranching, deforestation, global warming and so on) and the effects these have on the environment. They can also write off to wildlife protection societies for further information.

Assessing learning outcomes

Do the children understand the reasons why there are zoos and wildlife protection centres? Can they explain what an endangered species is and why the loss of a particular breed threatens the health of the environment? Are the children able to express their views on whether zoos and wildlife parks and so on are a good or a bad thing as far as the environment is concerned?

What's on the other side of the hedge?

1 hour 50 mins

Learning objectives
• Understand the environmental importance of hedgerows.
• Understand the implications associated with the loss of natural hedgerows (loss of habitat and ecosystems for insects and birds, soil erosion, use of man-made materials and problems with waste and sustainability).
• Identify creatures that live in or near hedgerows.

Lesson organisation
Initial class discussion; visit to the locality near school; follow up-class discussion; plenary.

Vocabulary
hedgerow
fencing
railings
ecosystems
habitats
flora
fauna

What you need and preparation

A local area close to school where there is a variety of hedges and fences – wooden panels, shrubs, iron railings and so on. Gather together a collection of reference books on trees and hedgerow flora and fauna. You will also need clip boards, writing materials, gloves (to pick up litter), bags (for collecting litter) and copies of photocopiable page 126.

What to do

Introduction
20 mins Talk to the children about all the different sorts of fencing and hedging they can name – wooden fences, natural hedgerows, iron railings and so on. Can they name any insects or creatures that live in, under or near hedgerows? Why are hedgerows important to birds? Give the children some time to browse through the reference books or find information on the Internet to familiarise themselves with types of trees, hedgerow plants, creatures and insects. Let the children talk about the books and share the information with a friend.

Development
1 hour Tell the children that you are going to take them out on a 'hedgerow detectives walk'. Before you go, divide the class into three groups. Explain to the children that during the walk each group is going to concentrate on finding out different types of information.

● *Group 1* Survey different kinds of fencing and hedging, for example wooden fences, natural hedgerows, iron railings or low brick walls. They should keep a tally of fences and hedges as they walk around using photocopiable page 126.

● *Group 2* Wearing the protective gloves, spot and collect litter found on, in or near fences and hedges. They should bring bottles, cans and wrappers back to the classroom.

● *Group 3* Look for clues to detect wildlife living in hedgerows such as webs, prints, trails, droppings on leaves and so on. Keep a tally of wildlife clues found using photocopiable page 126.

Plenary

30 mins Back in the classroom, discuss the findings from each task group. What conclusions can the children draw about the different types of hedging and fencing – which type is most common? What evidence was found to suggest which creatures might be living in or near hedgerows? How much litter was collected and what problems might this cause for small animals, insects and birds? What implications are there for the environment if most of the fencing is made of wood, concrete or metal?

Ask the children to suggest ideas for encouraging more people to plant hedges. They could, for example, write to the local council suggesting they plant more hedges along roads and in parks and so on. Or would a local garden centre consider running special offers on hedge shrubs and plants? Can the children think of reasons why people might prefer man-made fences to natural hedges (maintenance, slow growing when they want immediate privacy and so on)?

Differentiation

Allow the children a degree of choice when allocating the class to their groups. It is helpful if the children conducting the survey and keeping a tally can be relied upon and feel confident with data handling.

Younger children will need more guidance during the walk as to what to look for in and around hedges and fences to detect evidence of wildlife.

Older and more able children can go on to look at the environmental history of hedgerows and the relationship for example between the use of big machines, intensive farming and the loss of hedgerows.

Assessing learning outcomes

Are the children able to give reasons why natural hedgerows are an important part of a healthy environment? Can the children identify the kinds of animals, birds and insects that live in natural hedgerows and say why litter is a threat to some of these smaller creatures?

ICT opportunities
● The children could record aspects of their hedgerow detective work in a simple database.
● Give the children the opportunity to take photographs of their evidence for example different types of hedges and litter.

Think global –
act local

1 hour Which charity?

Learning objectives
• Experience the idea of helping people and their communities, animals and the environment through charity.
• See how the democratic process works when collective decisions need to be made.
• To become familiar with the works and aims of a range of charities.

Lesson organisation
Initial class discussion; group work; plenary.

Vocabulary
charity
voluntary
organisation
donation
contribution
aims

What you need and preparation

Gather together any information you can collect from local and national charities, especially those related to environmental issues, such as leaflets, newspaper and magazine advertisements. You will also need a local telephone directory and access to the Internet.

What to do

10 mins Introduction

Explain to the children that you think it would be a good idea if as a class you 'adopted a charity.' Can they tell you what a charity is? What charities do they already know about, such as Greenpeace, the RSPCA, Friends of the Earth, the Worldwide Fund for Nature and so on? Discuss with the children the literature you have collected and talk about what the various charities aim to do, why they need more help and why they need to advertise.

List on the board or a flip chart the names of as many charities as the children can think of. List these under different headings, for example those dealing with animals, those focusing specifically on the environment or those working with children. Can the children tell you which of these charities are international and which ones work only in Britain?

Tell the children that you would like them to work together to decide which charity they would like to support.

30 mins Development

Divide the class into five groups and give each a specific research task as follows. Encourage those children using the Internet to search by using key words such as environmental organisations, charities UK, wildlife, conservation, pollution.

● *Group 1* Using local directories, find out and list the names, addresses and telephone numbers of local charities that have been set up to help local causes, for example projects to help senior citizens, young children, animals or those which are trying to raise money to maintain historic buildings.

● *Group 3* Using the Internet and leaflets provided, find out and list the names of British charities that have been set up to support causes in Britain, for example the RSPCA or the National Trust.

● *Group 2* Using the Internet and leaflets provided, find out and list British charities that are international, in that they support projects in countries outside Britain, for example Oxfam, Fair Trade or Save the Children.

● *Group 4* Use the Internet to research which charities are specifically set up to support aspects of the environment, for example the Wildfowl and Wetlands Trust and Friends of the Earth.

● *Group 5* Investigate charities that work for and on behalf of children and/or animals.

20 mins Plenary

Ask each group to share its findings with the rest of the class. Discuss which charities they are most interested in – are these to support local, national or international projects, the environment, children or animals for example? Have a show of hands to whittle the list down to three favourite charities.

Explain to the children that they may not have enough information to make a fair decision at this stage. How will they find out more? You could agree that e-mails, letters or faxes could be sent to your top three charities asking for more information.

Once you have obtained the extra information you need, use subsequent sessions to have a class vote on which charity you will support and the form this support will take. You could draw up a plan of action and decide what to do first. It may be, for example, that the children decide to donate a small amount of their pocket money to your chosen charity on a regular basis, or that they would like to have a raffle or book sale and so on. Would they like to involve the rest of the school in any way?

Differentiation

This activity lends itself to participation on many different levels and provides learning opportunities for children of all different abilities. The older or more able children could use the Internet to research charities, printing out the home page and any other interesting information from their websites.

Younger or less able children may find it easier to focus their research on a charity they already know something about such as the RSPCA or Save the Children. They can then design posters or fact sheets to encourage people to support it.

Assessing learning outcomes

Can the children find out about local, national and environmental charities and say why they would like to support them? Can they make the links between charities and the well being of the environment and people in difficulty? Can they can work together to reach an informed view on particular charities and made a democratic decision?

Building healthy communities

Helping children to understand the nature of communities and the benefits of building and maintaining healthy ones are key strands of both the PSHE and Citizenship curriculum. The main aims of this chapter are to introduce children to the idea of communities and to help them understand how inter-related the various groups that make up a community are.

To build up an understanding of the way individuals and groups depend on each other, the children are asked to look initially at their own school as a community. From there the children are asked to consider the different types of jobs and services that need to be carried out in the local community in order that those living in that community can lead safe, fulfilled lives. There is an emphasis on taking the children out into the local community to make observations at first hand and to identify areas where facilities and provision could be improved – perhaps in making roads safer or thinking about special needs groups. Activities also include opportunities for bringing visitors from the local community into the classroom and for making your school more attractive to visitors.

The community is something the children may take for granted – for them, this is where they live, where they go to school, meet their friends, go shopping and so on. Understanding how all these activities are facilitated and maintained may be something children of this age have never really thought about before. Yet understanding how communities work is an essential first step towards feeling a sense of belonging, ownership and respect.

It is increasingly difficult to feel a sense of community in modern society. Many people live in one place and work in another – maybe doing their shopping on the way home at an out of town shopping centre where it's easier to park. Local shops are often used for emergency supplies only and this has a significant impact on the local economy as well as on the way community groups relate to each other. Making children aware of what has to happen to maintain their communities is one of the first steps towards healthy participation in those communities. Without this understanding and respect, young people may feel as if they don't really belong anywhere, which in turn can lead to problematic behaviour. Linked to this concept of community identity is the idea of rules. All communities need rules so that everyone knows what is expected of them and which kinds of activities are socially unacceptable.

The two units around which activities are designed in this chapter are called 'working together' and 'something for everyone.' Together these units encompass most of the main elements of what we mean by 'community'. The children are introduced to the concept of democracy and can practise voting in a class election. They are asked to consider the impact of greed on communities and to think about maintaining local environments.

These activities reflect the elements of the National Curriculum non-statutory guidelines which state that pupils should be taught: 'Why and how rules and laws are made and enforced, why different rules are needed in different situations and how to take part in making and changing rules' and 'To explore how the media present information'.

Working together

This unit aims to help children to understand how local communities knit together. Communities are complex structures in which people, live, learn and work together. For children, the community in which they live and learn is just there, something they rarely think about as an issue in its own right. Yet learning to live in a community is perhaps the most crucial of all the life skills.

This unit along with the second unit in this chapter, 'Something for everyone', is closely linked to the requirements to teach children about citizenship. The subject of democracy, voting procedures and local government is introduced and there are opportunities for the children to take part in debates and discussions and make democratic decisions.

The activities in this unit are designed to encourage the children to investigate and reflect on how their local communities actually work to protect the needs and interests of the people that live in them. The activities are based on the following themes:
● the jobs and roles required by a community to protect its inhabitants
● the need for communities to have rules in order to manage behaviour
● local provision
● the school as a community.

Because this chapter is all about the community, it makes sense to take the children out into the local community to investigate what's there and also to invite community members into the classroom. This emphasises the interpersonal relationship building that is an essential part of healthy communities.

With increasing concerns about pupil behaviour and the impact of negative attitudes on local communities, it is essential for children to understand why rules are necessary.

UNIT: Working together

Enquiry questions	Learning objectives	Teaching activities	Learning outcomes	Cross-curricular links
Who makes things happen around here?	• Understand the sorts of jobs that people do in the community.	Work with a photocopiable sheet to identify day and night-time jobs and investigate their role in the community. Present ideas as information cards.	*Children:* • know what is meant by a community • understand what jobs are necessary to support a community	ICT: using a word-processing program to redraft information cards.
Why do communities need rules?	• Learn why communities need rules. • Identify rules in different community settings. • Express a considered opinion on rules that operate around them.	Teacher-led discussion to introduce the idea of rules. Define rules in different settings. Work with a photocopiable sheet to devise a list of essential rules.	• explain why rules are necessary • identify different sorts of rules	English: presenting a view in an appropriate tone of voice to a particular audience.
Would you like to join us?	• Find out about a particular community-based job. • Meet a community member and discuss their role in supporting the community.	Based on a visitor coming into the classroom. Children have opportunity to prepare and ask questions.	• describe the visitor's job • say how this job supports the community	English: writing letters and invitations; speaking and listening; asking questions.
What's the shopping centre all about?	• Understand through a local 'survey' what shops, services and food outlets operate in the local community. • Understand the importance of these services and shops to the well-being and comfort of the local community.	Based on a visit to the local shopping centre. Identify what is available locally and why they are located there.	• identify different sorts of local shops and services • suggest additional shops, services and food outlets that would benefit the community	Geography: surveying the local environment.
Is our school a community too?	• Understand who makes up the school community. • Appreciate the inter-dependency of groups in the school community.	Work on a definition of community. Identify different groups within the school community. Complete a 'community web'.	• define 'community' • identify school groups.	English: word level literacy – defining and understanding the meaning of words.

Resources
Reference material on jobs within the local community, material on school rules, competition entry forms from newspapers, magazines and so on, clipboards, a camera.

Display
Notices describing school rules.

① Who makes things happen around here?
1 hour

What you need and preparation

Gather together a selection of reference resources about a range of community occupations – those jobs which impact directly on everyone's life such as doctors, police officers, nurses, shopkeepers or rescue services. You will also need individual copies of photocopiable pages 127 and 128.

What to do

10 mins Introduction

Explain to the children what we mean by 'community' (a group of people that live, learn or work together). Ask the children what sorts of jobs people do that help us to live comfortably and safely in the community. It may help them to pinpoint the jobs and services which impact on the community directly if the children think in terms of 'people who help us'. Explain that they are going to be researchers to find out more about these community based jobs and how important they are.

40 mins Development

Give each child a copy of photocopiable page 127 and explain to them how they fill it in. Tell the class they have about 10 minutes for this. After this time, call the class back together and spend a few minutes talking about the sorts of jobs they have recorded.

Give each child a copy of photocopiable page 128 and ask them to work in pairs or small groups to make information cards about particular community-based jobs. Let them choose the ones they are particularly interested in. Discuss where they will find their information (books, the Internet and so on). The children's information cards should contain the job title, what it entails, who it helps the community and what we can do to help the people doing these jobs (for example not making unnecessary emergency calls, telling the police if you see anything suspicious or dangerous and so on).

10 mins Plenary

Share the information gathered by different groups and discuss how all these different jobs and services make up the support we need in our communities. Then children may like to put their information cards together as a useful resource pack.

Differentiation

Younger and less able children can choose one particular community job, such as a fire officer or nurse, about which they already know something. They could also write an account of a visit to the doctor's or a stay in hospital, for example, or they may have a relative who has a community-based job about whom they could tell a story.

Older and more able children can write more detailed information on their cards such as how long it takes to train in a certain community-based job and the hours they work. They could also write a 'day in the life of…' for the job on their card.

Assessing learning outcomes

Can the children describe what is meant by a community and name some of the occupations and services that are needed to support the health and well being of communities? Do they understand the community role of specific occupations, such as refuse collectors, shopkeepers and rescue services?

Learning objectives
• Understand the sorts of jobs and services that peole do in the community.

Lesson organisation
Whole class discussion; individual follow up work; plenary.

Vocabulary
occupations
jobs
community
support
services

ICT opportunity
Ask the children to redraft their cards on the computer. Encourage them to incorporate simple artwork into their cards using artwork software.

(1 hour) Why do communities need rules?

Learning objectives
• Understand the need for communities to have rules and agreed codes of conduct.
• Understand rules which are particular to specific community settings such as home, school and the local community.
• Express a considered opinion on rules that operate around them.

Lesson organisation
Introductory class discussion; individual reinforcement activity; follow-up; plenary.

Vocabulary
rules
regulations
agreement
conduct
fairness
honesty
protection

What you need and preparation

Gather together a selection of any display materials you have in school relating to rules, good behaviour, or attitudes towards others, for example notices reminding children how to move around the school, how to behave in the school hall during lunch, how to take turns using the computer and so on. Gather together some competition entry forms from newspapers, magazines or cereal packets that list rules and conditions. You will also need a piece of A3 paper for each child. You will need copies of photocopiable page 129 for the follow-up activity.

What to do

(20 mins) Introduction

Ask the class what rules are and why we have them. Discuss your stimulus materials and ask the children to tell you about other sorts of rules they know about – at home, school and in the community. Establish that there are many different sorts of rules but that all rules state how people are expected to behave in particular settings – during games, as we move around school or socialise in the community.

Ask the children to think about what life would be like if there were no rules. For example, what would a game of rounders be like if there were no rules? Imagine what would happen if everyone was allowed to just take what they wanted or could hurt people if they felt like it.

(30 mins) Development

Remind the children about different types of rules that operate in different community settings, especially at school, home and in their local community. Which rules, if any, do they consider to be unfair – why?

Give each child a piece of A3 paper, folded into three like a concertina. Tell the children that they should write 'Home rules' as a heading on the first section, 'School rules' on the second section and 'Community rules' on the third. Tell the children that you would like them to write and illustrate the rules they have to abide by in each setting. For example, under 'Home rules' they might write, 'If I don't eat my main course, I'm not allowed any pudding' or 'no television after 9pm'.

(10 mins) Plenary

Discuss with the whole class what sorts of conclusions they have come to about the fairness – or otherwise – of rules. Ask the children to explain why rules are a necessary part of living in communities. Talk about the sorts of positive things the children themselves can do if they feel something is unfair and needs to be changed. Their ideas could include, for example, talking to an adult about it when they feel angry or upset, writing a letter to the people/organisation concerned, set up a school council and so on.

Differentiation

Younger children may find the follow-up activity quite challenging because it is rather more

abstract than thinking about school rules or the things they are allowed to do at home for example. They will, however, be able to identify and talk about examples of unfairness they have experienced in their own lives and retell the event as a story to share with others, or make a drawing with simple captions.

Older and more able children can give additional comments on their concertina book of rules such as whether they think a particular rule is fair, if they think it works or new rules they think should be added to any of the three sections.

Assessing learning outcomes

Do the children understand the reasons why communities have rules? Can they list rules that apply in different community settings? Are they able to express an opinion about particular rules and give reasons why they consider them fair, sensible and practical?

Follow-up activity
Give the children photocopiable page 129 which asks them to come up with five rules that they consider essential for all communities. They are asked to imagine they are castaways on a desert island where resources are limited. Which do they consider to be the most important rules in order that everyone will be able to work and life together safely and comfortably?

Would you like to join us?

What you need and preparation

Organise a visit from a volunteer from the local community who has an interesting or unusual job working as part of the local community, for example a local chef, rescue worker, leisure centre manager or a crafts person such as carpenter or stone mason. It may be that one of the children in the class knows someone – perhaps a member of their family who is in such a job – and may be able to ask them to visit the class. If possible involve the children in the decision about who is going to come and visit them. Which jobs are the children most interested in finding out about?

What to do

30 mins Introduction

Tell the children they will be inviting a visitor into the classroom to talk about their job. Explain a little about what your visitor's job entails and why it is important to the whole community – police officer, doctor, the local vet, a plumber and so on. Ask the children to each write down three questions they would like to ask their visitor. The children could put these in order according to which one they would most like to know the answer to. When the children have finished their lists, discuss their questions as a class. If possible, organise it so that each child has a different question to ask the visitor. Many of the children will have come up with the same questions and it may be necessary to reallocate questions around the class.

Learning objectives
• Gain a deeper understanding of a particular community based occupation.
• Meet a community-based worker in order to discuss his or her job.

Lesson organisation
Introductory session to prepare the children for the visit; a class visit; follow-up to the visit.

Vocabulary
occupation
expert
specialism
skill
visitor
courtesy

Give the children an opportunity to practise asking their questions – they could work in pairs taking turns to ask and listen. Remind the children about asking their questions politely, speaking clearly and really listening to the answer.

45 mins Development

Before your visitor arrives, ask for a volunteer to practise saying thank you at the end.

During the visit give the children plenty of time to ask their questions.

15 mins **Plenary**
Discuss the information you have learned from the visitor about the job they do and how it helps the community as a whole. Would the children like to do that job when they are older?

Differentiation

Younger or less confident children may prefer to have their question written out so that they can refer to it if they feel nervous or forget what they meant to say. Keep the visit shorter with the younger age group and if possible ask your visitor to bring any tools of trade or visual aids.

Older and more able children could research more about other community jobs related to your visitor's occupation for example linkages between the rescue services. They could also write an account of the visit for the school newsletter or as a report to the school governors.

Assessing learning outcomes

Can the children explain what the job of your visitor entails? Do the children understand how your visitor's job relates to the rest of the local community?

Follow-up activity
Ask the children to write a thank you letter to your visitor, telling him or her how they used the information they learned that day.

---

2 hours 30 mins ## What's the shopping centre all about?

What you need and preparation

Organise a class visit to a local shopping centre. You will need sufficient adult helpers to accompany you on the visit. You will also need clipboards, writing materials, a camera and copies of photocopiable page 130. Make all the necessary arrangements for taking the children out of school for two or three hours.

Learning objectives
• Survey and reflect on the shops and services that are provided in their local communities.
• Understand the importance of these services and shops to the well being and comfort of the local community.

Lesson organisation
Preparatory class discussion; class visit to local shopping centre; class and individual follow up work; plenary.

Vocabulary
services
utilities
goods
local provision

What to do

20 mins **Introduction**
Explain to the children that you will be going out to the local shopping centre to find out about the sorts of goods and services that are available locally. Make sure that the children understand that 'services' in this context includes things like repair shops, utility offices and suppliers. Which shops and services can the children already name?

Tell the children that during the visit you would like them to find out:
● what sorts of shops there are and the products they sell
● the kinds of services there are in the centre such as repair workshops or electricity offices, photocopying services, electricity offices and so on
● how many restaurants there are, including fast food outlets.

Explain that you would also like the children to think about how easy or difficult it was to find their way around the centre. Did they notice any special facilities for people with disabilities or learning difficulties such as wheelchair access, accessible lifts, public announcements to help the visually

impaired and so on? Give each child a copy of photocopiable page 130 to take with them on the visit. Go through the page with them making sure they understand how to record their information.

Development

Go on the visit and help the children to record their data to use later. Take photographs as you walk around the shopping centre.

Plenary

When you return to the classroom discuss the children's findings. Was there anything that surprised them – for example the small number of repair shops or the large number of restaurants? What other kinds of shops and service would the children like to have locally?

Differentiation

Older children can make deductions from their survey data such as why shops and services are located in particular places. Who might use any specialist services and suppliers such as computer or camera shops? How much has the shopping centre changed in the last 20 years? What reasons can they think of for these changes (advances in technology, more out of town shopping, access to transport, high rents and so on)?

Assessing learning outcomes

Can the children explain why certain facilities, shops and services are located in the centre? Can they describe how access to these shops and services is important to the whole community? Can the children suggest what other services and shops would be useful to their local community?

**ICT
opportunity**
The children can set up a simple database to record their findings. They can go on to investigate if their shopping centre has more shops, restaurants or repair services for example.

CHAPTER 4
BUILDING HEALTHY COMMUNITIES

Working together

① Is our school a community too?
1 hour

Learning objectives
• Understand the concept of a community by looking at the people that make up your school community.
• Appreciate that the school community is made up of people doing different jobs, and that these roles are equally important for the well-being of the whole-school community as it works together.

Lesson organisation
Whole-class introductory discussion; individual reinforcement activity; small group follow-up work; plenary.

Vocabulary
community
roles
administration
office
staff
governors
pupils
teachers
support

What you need and preparation
You will need copies of photocopiable page 131.

What to do

⑮ Introduction
15 mins

Establish with the children what we mean by the word 'community' and try to come up with a class definition. For example, 'A community is a collection of people living, working and learning together.' The children may find it helpful to think about how animals live in communities too. Discuss how we can regard communities as a natural way of protecting the needs of individuals within groups. The children will probably know about prides of lions, ant colonies and packs of wolves and so on. Talk about how these animal communities look after their young, teach them how to survive in the world and how to find and produce food and protect each other from danger.

Ask the children to think about school as a community. How do the different people in the school work together to make sure everyone is safe and happy? Can the children name the different groups of people that make up their school community – pupils, teachers, office staff, lunchtime supervisors, cleaning staff, governors, parents? Ask the children to think about the different jobs these people do and talk about how these roles are dependent on each other, and fit together to make the whole school work well together.

㉟ Development
35 mins

Give each child a copy of photocopiable page 131. Talk through the page with them, drawing on your introductory discussion. Ask the children to fill in the gaps on the school to create a community web.

Discuss the children's outcomes and ask them to work in pairs or small groups to make a list of the jobs done by people in each section of the web. For example, under the section called *office staff*, they could write: answer the phone, write letters, help the headteacher, check the registers, look after the money and so on.

Some children will be able to go on to make other connections. For example the links between the headteacher and the teachers and the secretary. Discuss all these possibilities with the children as they are working and help them to see that in fact the school community is quite a complex web of relationships – each dependent on the other.

⑩ Plenary
10 mins

Recap on the idea of the school as a community and that it will work best if the different people in school understand what other people have to do as part of their job. What sorts of

things can go wrong in school? How does the school community work out its problems – through discussion, making decisions to change something or introducing new rules, talking to parents and so on? Remind the children about the times when the community – parents, local politicians and businesses – have helped the school. For example, the parents-teachers association may have raised money for new equipment, or a local business may have sponsored a major school event.

Differentiation

Younger and less able children will be doing quite well if they can list just two or three tasks under each heading. They will find some sections easier than others, for example they may not realise that parents are part of the school community too. For these children it will help them to see how these different groups work together if they talk through with you the sequence of their school day thinking about who is involved at each stage. For example, 'my dad makes sure I get to school on time, my teacher helps me to do my work, the lunch time supervisors look after me at lunch times…'

Older and more able children can go on to think and write about some of the problems these different groups may have, for example 'it must be very hard for my teacher to help us with our work if we are all being noisy'. They could offer some suggestions for helping different people in the school to do their job, for example, 'it would help the caretaker if we took off our muddy boots before we come indoors.'

> **Follow-up activity**
> Invite members of the school community to talk to the children about their job. For example, the headteacher could come and talk about his or her role in the school. The children will see the headteacher regularly and know that he or she is in charge of the community, but they may only have a very hazy idea about what the rest of the job is all about.

Assessing learning outcomes

Can the children define what a community is and explain how a community looks after individuals within it? Are the children able to identify the different groups of people that make up the school community? Can the children clearly express their views about how the school community can work together to make things even better?

Something for everyone

This unit further explores the interdependency between different groups and individuals within a community. The themes and activities are closely related to Citizenship Education, and can be used to introduce children at Key Stage 2 to some of the major themes relating to living with others in a community.

The themes covered in this unit are:

● **democracy and the voting system**

These activities are designed to help the children to understand democracy as a core aspect of living in healthy communities. They are given the opportunity to have a real-life debate and take part in a class vote through a secret ballot – thus mirroring the system used in local and general elections.

● **local community provision**

The children are encouraged to investigate and reflect on the level and type of services and facilities available in their local community. They can explore further to come up with ideas for additional services and provision. In this way the children will begin to feel part of the community and actively involved in it.

● **road safety**

The issue of road safety is included in this unit because moving around safely in the community is a basic human right. As children of this age begin to ride their bicycles on the roads or go out to play with their friends at the park, road safety procedures need to be reinforced regularly.

● **greed and its impact on the community**

The effect that greed has on the local community is something which can easily be overlooked, and yet greed is often at the centre of criminal activity and disharmony. At this stage the children can easily relate greed to their own experiences, and here they are invited to suggest strategies for dealing with it.

● **community and the environment**

The final activity is presented as a board game called 'going green'. The idea is to reinforce the main environmental subjects that impact hugely on communities – and for the children to have fun at the same time.

UNIT: Something for everyone

Enquiry questions	Learning objectives	Teaching activities	Learning outcomes	Cross-curricular links
Does your vote count?	• Learn about democracy and voting. • Voice opinions in a reasoned way. • Listen to and respect the views of others.	• Organise a debate and hold a class election.	• Know what an election is. • Express a reasoned opinion.	English: speaking and listening from a reasoned standpoint.
Is everyone safe?	• Understand the importance of keeping safe in the community. • Identify road safety devices in their local community.	• Class visit to local town or city.	• Understand road safety. • Suggest safety improvements locally.	Science: health and safety; Technology: planning.
What do we need in our community?	• Learn that the community is composed of different groups of people. • Learn about the community's collective needs. • Investigate the local facilities.	• Work in groups to investigate the needs of different community groups.	• Recognise different community groups and their needs. • Can suggest additional provision.	Geography: improving the local environment.
What do we do about greed?	• Think about the negative impact of greed on the community. • Suggest strategies for dealing with greed as a community issue.	• Work with a photocopiable page to suggest strategies for dealing with greed.	• Understand why greed is bad for communities. • Can suggest ways of tackling greed.	English: speaking and listening; writing short stories.
Are we part of the community?	• Understand the significance of community and environmental issues.	• Play a board game to reinforce learning about communities and the environment.	• Can identify major environmental issues and relate these to their community and personal reponsibilities.	Geography: environmental issues applied locally.

Resources
Road safety equipment, for example cycle helmets, luminous armbands, lights and so on, local telephone directory, stories about greed, for example *The Selfish Giant* by Oscar Wilde, dice and counters.

Display
Road safety posters.

CHAPTER 4
BUILDING HEALTHY COMMUNITIES

Something for everyone

① (1 hour) Does your vote count?

Learning objectives
• Learn some of the basic concepts about democracy and voting.
• Voice opinions in a reasoned way.
• Listen to and respect the views of others.

Lesson organisation
Initial class discussion; two groups to prepare the debate; individual voting; plenary.

Vocabulary
democracy
voting
election
ballot
polling card
majority
opinions
reasoning
fairness
tolerance

What you need and preparation

You will need a copy of the class register and a ballot box (a carton with a slot cut in the top for the children to 'post' their votes). Create voting slips with the motion and the opposing motion on them with clear space beside for the cross. You will also need copies of photocopiable page 132.

What to do

15 mins **Introduction**
Introduce the idea of voting and the rights of individuals to have their say by asking the children to think about all the different ways that decisions are made at school, at home and in the local community. What, for example, as the teacher do you do if you want to find out if the class would rather finish a piece of work now or do something else and finish it tomorrow? How are decisions made at home? Do their parents or carers ask their opinion about where to go on holiday or what to have for dinner? Do the children know how a new MP is chosen or a new Prime Minister?

Explain to the children what democracy is. Tell them that they are going to practise having an election and voting on something which will affect the lives of everyone in the school community.

Show the children the polling card (photocopiable page 132) and explain to them that in local and general elections, people over the age of 18 must take these cards with them to the polling station when they vote. Hand out the cards to the children and ask them to fill them in.

40 mins **Development**
Tell the children that they are going to vote in a class election. Explain that first there is going to be a class debate about the subject at the end of which they will all get a chance to vote in a 'secret ballot'.

Give the children the subject of the debate, for example 'this class thinks they should be allowed to bring their pets to school'. There may in fact be a real-life debate going on in the school or in the local community, such as building a bypass or introducing a new school uniform. If so, you could tap into this debate to give an extra sense of realism.

Divide the children into two groups – one for the motion and one against. Ask each group to come up with four well-reasoned points to support their side of the argument. Explain that they will need to develop these points and use them later in the class debate to persuade 'the voters' to agree with them. Each group should elect a spokesperson to present their case. Allow the groups about 15 minutes to come up with their four points. Next ask the children to think up a question each that they would like to ask the spokesperson from the other group.

When the two groups are ready, ask the two spokespersons to present their case to the rest of class. Once the spokespersons have finished, allow time for the other children to ask questions of the two spokespersons.

Carry out your secret ballot. Ask the children to bring their polling cards up to a desk where one of the children has been given the responsibility of marking their names off against the class register and handing out the ballot papers. The children can then mark their ballot papers and post them in the box.

Ask the children to help you to count the vote, as a useful way of reinforcing number work. Can they think of ways of making it easier such as putting the voting slips into piles of 5 or 10?

Something for
everyone

5 mins Plenary

Announce the winner of the class election. Talk about how in a democracy, once a 'majority decision' has been made, it is the responsibility of all members of the community to abide by the decision (although this may not include actually bringing the family donkey to school!)

Differentiation

The younger children may find this easier as a circle time activity where you can invite individual contributions and guide the process. They should, however, still be asked to show their choices with a cross (X) on a piece of paper.

Older children will be able to take more control of the process themselves – indeed it is an ideal opportunity to reinforce the idea of toleration towards others, letting others have their say without interruption and so on. With this older age group you can also let them take responsibility for marking off the voters' names on the register as they hand in their polling cards, appointing a chairperson to run the whole proceedings, having a team of tellers who must count the votes twice and so on. Can the children work out and announce the 'majority vote'?

Assessing learning outcomes

Do the children have a clearer idea about how the voting system works? Can they identify the vocabulary involved in voting? Can the children present their opinions in a reasoned, logical and polite way?

 # Is everyone safe?

What you need and preparation

Gather together a selection of road safety posters and a small collection of road safety equipment, for example cycle helmets, luminous armbands, lights and so on. Find a map of the vicinity around your school that is suitable for use on an overhead projector. Organise the support of adult helpers to accompany you on your walk round the area. You will also need clipboards.

What to do

15 mins Introduction

Ask the children to think about how safe the local community is for the people who live there or for any people who are travelling through it. Ask the children to describe some of the dangers of moving around the local town or city centre. Ask them to consider transport, pedestrians, older people, people with special needs, young children and animals. What road safety devices can the children recall seeing in the centre of town – for example, traffic lights, pelican crossings, one-way streets, pedestrian areas, cycle paths and so on? Discuss how these actually improve safety and how they should be used. Remind the children about the additional dangers for cyclists and pedestrians when they travel after dark or in difficult weather conditions. Show the children the safety equipment you have collected together and stress the importance of using it.

Explain to the children that you are all going out on a community safety check to see how safe their community is and to suggest ways of making it safer.

Learning objectives
• Understand the importance of keeping safe in the community, especially as a cyclist or pedestrian.
• See at first hand the sorts of road safety devices which are in place in their local community and look for ways of making it even safer.

Lesson organisation
Initial teacher-led, whole-class introduction; class visit to the local town or city centre; whole-class follow-up; plenary.

Vocabulary
safety
pedestrians
pelican crossing
traffic
protection

ICT opportunities
• Ask the children to use the Internet to find the websites for organisations that focus on safety such as ROSPA.
• The children could make a tape recording for a person who has impaired vision to teach them how to use a pelican crossing.

Follow-up activity
Ask the children to investigate other aspects of community safety such as making our homes more secure, reducing accidents in the home or looking after the oldest and youngest members of the community.

Development

2 hours Take the children out on a walk around the local area. While you're out with the children draw their attention to the safety equipment and devices you come across. Why do the children think they are located there? Ask them to notice particularly busy areas outside shops, close to bus or train stations and residential areas. Ask the children:

● what special care has been taken to ensure people's safety in those areas?
● where are the cycle paths or subways?
● how could safety be improved in different parts of the centre?

Back in the classroom, ask the children to recall where the busiest areas were and whether they think these areas could be made safer for the whole community. For example, should there be more pedestrian only places or pelican crossings? Using the local map on the overhead projector, plot these busy areas and other places that could be made safer.

Plenary

15 mins As a class, sum up all the road safety issues you have identified. Decide together if the children would like to present their findings and ideas in a form that would help others, such as in a poster or leaflet.

Can the children suggest ways of helping to make sure their ideas for improvements could be put into action? For example, could they write to the local council or MP.

Differentiation

To reinforce the idea of road safety, young children could practise procedures for crossing the road, getting ready to go on a cycle ride or what to do at a pelican crossing. You could ask them to draw and label a sequence showing how they can help older or disabled people to cross a busy street. They could also make labels for the safety wear you have in your stimulus collection.

Older and more able children could write letters to the local council or MP suggesting safety improvements in the community. They could also write letters and articles for the local paper outlining their concerns and ideas.

Assessing learning outcomes

Can the children demonstrate that they understand how road safety devices and procedures work? Can they identify particular safety concerns in especially busy locations in their local community? Can they make informed suggestions for improving the safety of the whole community as people move around from place to place?

Something for
everyone

What do we need in our community?

(1 hour)

What you need and preparation

You will need a collection of local telephone directory and copies of photocopiable page 133.

What to do

Introduction

(15 mins) Ask the children to think about the different groups of people that make up their local community. Begin by thinking about different age groups, babies and young children, teenagers, adults and senior citizens. What other sorts of groups are there in the community? These might include special interest groups, religious communities, a prison population and so on.

Explain to the children that they will be working in groups to consider the needs of these various groups and what facilities are provided for them in the community.

Development

(35 mins) Divide the children into groups of around four or five. Tell them that each group is going to investigate the facilities needed by a certain group of people in the communty. Give each group a copy of photocopiable page 133 on which to record their ideas. Give each group a specific task as follows:

● *Group 1* What facilities do children need? (Somewhere safe to play, nursery schools, bicycle paths and so on.)
● *Group 2* What facilities do senior citizens need? (Pelican crossings, somewhere to meet their friends, special care facilities and so on.)
● *Group 3* What facilities do people with special needs need? (Wheelchair ramps, paths along busy roads, people to help them move around more easily and so on).
● *Group 4* What facilities do special interest groups (clubs, crafts, people and ethnic minorities) need? (Workshop facilities, somewhere to practise their religion, specialist shops selling food free from animal prodcts and so on.)

Explain to the children that they should use the local directories as well as their knowledge of the local area find out whether the facilites they have suggested are available. Tell the children that if they are unable to find out whether these facilities are available using the resources provided, they should indicate this on their sheet and suggest ways in which they could find out this information.

Plenary

(10 mins) Share the groups' findings and discuss how many of the facilities suggested are already provided in their communities. Can they think of ways in which they could help to bring about improved facilities for those groups which seem to be under-provided for? You could invite a town planner to visit the class to tell the children about some of the practical problems involved in providing some facilities and what plans there are for the future.

Differentiation

With younger children it is a good idea to narrow the focus slightly. Ask them to make a list of the sorts of activities they like to do out of school hours, such as playing games with their friends, going to the cinema or riding their bicycles. How easily can they do these things near where they live? Ask them to suggest what else they would like to have nearby.

Older and more able children could take the concept of community provision and facilities a stage further by designing their dream town, showing how the different community groups would be catered for.

Learning objectives
● Learn that the community is composed of different groups of people – children, teenagers, the elderly and so on.
● Understand the idea of a community's collective needs.
● Investigate the local facilities and assess if these are adequate.

Lesson organisation
Initial class discussion; follow up group work; plenary.

Vocabulary
provision
facilities
senior citizens
special needs
special interest
groups
ideal

CHAPTER 4
BUILDING HEALTHY COMMUNITIES

Something for
everyone

Assessing learning outcomes

Are the children able to identify the different groups that make up their local community? Can they say what local facilities these groups need? Can they find out if and where these facilities are to be found in their local community? Can they suggest additional facilities that would be of benefit to local community?

① What do we do about greed?
hour

Learning objectives
• Think about greed as an aspect of community living and devise strategies for dealing with it.
• Relate stories and share experiences about greed and the effects it can have on other members of the community.

Lesson organisation
Initial class discussion; individual work; follow-up drama activities; plenary.

Vocabulary
greed
sharing
selfishness
problem solving

What you need and preparation

Story book about greed, for example The Selfish Giant, by Oscar Wilde. You will also need photocopiable page 134.

What to do

⑮ Introduction
mins

Introduce the idea of greed and what it means to the community by reading the story with the children. How did the characters show their greed? What effect did this have on the other characters? How was the problem sorted out in the end? Can the children recall and collect other stories about greed – either from their own experiences or from a book they have read?

Discuss with the children why greed can pose a threat to communities – if everyone simply took as much as they wanted there wouldn't be enough of everything to go round.

㉟ Development
mins

Give the children a copy of photocopiable page 134. They can work in pairs, small groups or individually. Ask them to show in the next sequence how the greed problem was dealt with. The first example of a child not sharing their sweets is one with which the children can readily identify. Encourage them to discuss with their partner what they would do about this kind of greed – perhaps they could draw a picture of two other children with speech bubbles saying, for example, 'Why are you being so greedy?' 'It would be nice if you shared those with us, we like sweets too.'

In the second example the family is shown enjoying their own wealth. In many ways there is nothing wrong with this. However, the children might draw a picture of the family giving something to charity, or doing some voluntary work.

⑩ Plenary
mins

Ask for volunteers to show and discuss their picture sequences to the restof the class. Ask the children to think about how the community could work out ways of persuading people to be less greedy and help those who are not so fortunate, or who would also like to share resources. For example, the children might suggest that the community writes letters or designs posters to persuade richer people to support the less well off through charity work, or using their homes to provide facilities for disadvantaged children.

Differentiation

Younger children could work with a partner to act out the first two frames of the story and show what happens next.

Older and more able children can add further frames and make their stories more complex. They could try writing short play scripts to act out later.

Something for
everyone

Assessing learning outcomes

Did the children understand the main messages of the story you read at the beginning of the activity? Can they explain why greed can be a major problem for a community? Have the children shown through their interpretations of the worksheet scenarios that they can think of strategies to deal with greed?

ICT opportunities
The children could make a story tape for a younger member of the family or another class called for example 'the little tape of greed'. This could consist of readings from story books such as *The Selfish Giant* or Aesop's Fables or from their own stories.

45 mins Are we part of the community?

What you need and preparation

You will need copies of photocopiable pages 135 and 136. You will also need dice and counters.

What to do

10 mins Introduction
Explain the game to the class, making sure they understand the rules. Tell the children to write down their scores as they go along, and add them up at the end. Explain that the game is finished when the first player reaches the forest (home). The winner is the player with the most points at the end of the game.

30 mins Development
Ask the children to work in pairs and hand out photocopiable pages 135 and 136 to them. The children play the game in pairs.

As the children are playing the game stop them from time to time to discuss the environmental issues that feature on some of the spaces.

5 mins Plenary
Discuss the environmental and community issues included in the game and ask the children to say one thing they know about each of them. Can they think of any other important environmental issues they would like to include?

Learning objectives
• Understand the main environmental issues and messages.
• Have fun learning about the environment.

Lesson organisation
Introductory session with the whole class; board game played in pairs; plenary.

Vocabulary
environment
conservation
sustainability
waste
recycling

Differentiation

The game can be easily adapted to suit the needs, ages and abilities of individual children. Some children will be able to make further extension boards for making the game longer or introducing further environmental issues.

To reinforce numeracy skills, older or more able children could play the game with two dice. They could be encouraged to make up their own scoring system, work with averages and probability.

Assessing learning outcomes

Did the children enjoy playing the game? Can they identify and explain the environmental issues incorporated in to the game?

Building a healthy future

The concept of 'future' is often quite problematic for young children to grasp. It is difficult for them to imagine, for example, what they might be doing when they are the same age as their parents, or what sort of job they might do when they leave school or college. Seven- to nine-year-olds are relatively powerless to change things or have a say in their own futures. However, if children are to make sensible decisions later on it is important that they learn strategies for dealing with the huge range of circumstances and relationships in which they will find themselves as teenagers and adults.

A healthy future largely depends on two things – the kinds of decisions individuals make about how they want to conduct their lives, and sustainable development. Thus the two units in this chapter aim to develop the children's skills in making positive, informed choices and also to alert them to the importance of managing the earth's natural resources. The activities ask children to think about the decision making process itself – how does one actually make a choice? Who would the children go to if they had a difficult decision to make?

The children are also asked to consider the sorts of choices they make as consumers and the power of advertising, and to look at ways of managing their own time. There are also opportunities to think about moral dilemmas and the sometimes uncomfortable decisions we all have to make from time to time, and also to express their hopes and dreams for the future.

The concept of sustainability is clearly crucial for a healthy future, and this is recognised in the non-statutory guidelines which state: 'Pupils should be taught that resources can be allocated in different ways and that these economic choices affect individuals, communities and the sustainability of the environment.'

Some of the themes introduced in Chapter 3: Building Healthy Environments are revisited here with the emphasis this time on what we need to do to ensure that resources are managed in such a way that there will be enough for future generations. The children are invited to think about the impact of technology on our present and future lives, and to find out about 'alternative technology'.

There are opportunities for extending the activities and themes into other areas of the curriculum, most notably literacy, numeracy, ICT and science.

Making choices

Making decisions is a process that many people find extremely difficult. Yet making the right choices is key to a healthy future. This unit is designed to help children think about some of the choices they will be expected to make in the future and how those decisions might be made.

The activities focus on the following themes:

● **the decision making process itself**

Learning how to make a decision takes a long time and we often make the wrong choices. Children also need to learn strategies for dealing with disappointment as well as with success. These activities offer opportunities for the children to practise those skills and strategies.

● **making choices as a consumer**

Today's school children are the consumers of the future. It is for this reason that activities introducing children to the notion of good consumerism have been included. The activities encourage children to think carefully before they buy things and to reflect on the impact of advertising and the media on their consumer choices.

● **time management**

Time management is also an important and often difficult skill to learn. Many employers complain that young people enter the market place with poor time management and organisational skills. Teaching these skills at Key Stage 2 helps to address this gap.

● **moral dilemmas and choices**

Helping children to reflect on moral issues is also an important aspect of building a healthy future. Children can be quite reactionary in their views and they will also come from a range of cultures each with its own moral or religious code. It follows that a degree of sensitivity is required when asking the children to talk about what is right and wrong. The main aim is to encourage the children to listen to the views of others without being judgmental or intolerant.

● **hopes and dreams**

The final activity in this unit is about the hopes and dreams the children have for their futures.

These themes can be considered as crucial life skills – skills that all the children will need in the future.

UNIT: Making choices

Enquiry questions	Learning objectives	Teaching activities	Learning outcomes	Cross-curricular links
How can we decide?	• Learn how to make decisions. • Understand the importance of decision-making in working towards a healthy future.	Discuss the sorts of decisions they make at school, at home and in the local community. Follow-up writing on 'difficult decisions'.	*Children:* • understand which decisions they find difficult • work towards a strategy for decision-making	English: extended writing.
Are you a good consumer?	• Understand the effects of advertising on consumers. • Develop strategies for making informed consumer decisions.	Investigate advertising material. Use photocopiable sheet to help them work out how to look beyond the advertising 'hype'.	• recognise that advertising exerts a powerful influence on consumers	English: writing own versions of advertisements.
Is your time well spent?	• Learn to make sensible informed choices about how to use time effectively. • Understand that time management is an important part of building a healthy future. • Learn to take responsibility for managing our time and organising ourselves.	Discuss how class members spend their time. Work out individual timetables to organise time.	• complete a timetable to guide time management • recognise which activities they can control and manage	[no link]
Right or wrong?	• Manage personal behaviour and decide what is 'right' or 'wrong'. • Make the connections between moral issues and good citizenship.	Introductory discussion. Work in pairs to portray solutions to moral dilemmas given on a photocopiable sheet.	• understand that an individual has choices about how to behave	English: predicting story endings and suggesting new versions.
What are our hopes and dreams?	• Consider the kinds of decisions they will need to make in the future. • Identify aspirations and what we have to do in order to achieve our hopes and dreams.	Discussion. Children work in pairs to explore their hopes and dreams.	• can describe their hopes and dreams • assess how to achieve them.	English: extended writing.

Resources
Writing and drawing materials, a range of advertising materials, examples of timetables, a selection of reference books about growing up.

 # How can we decide?

What you need and preparation
Writing and drawing materials.

What to do

Introduction
10 mins Introduce the idea of choices and decision making by asking the children to think about all the different decisions they have to make during the course of a normal day: *Shall I have another piece of toast for breakfast? Should I take my new game to school? Who shall I invite round to my house after school, what television programme shall I watch after supper?*

These are everyday choices and fairly easy decisions to make. Can the children remember a time when they had to make a more serious decision? Have they ever had to decide whether to tell an adult about something they have done that they know is wrong? Have they ever had to decide whether to do something they don't really want to do?

Development
30 mins Explain to the children that you would like them to think about the sorts of decisions and choices they make at home, at school and in their spare time. Who would they talk to if they had a difficult decision to make?

Give each child a piece of paper folded or divided into three sections. Ask the children to write the heading *Home choices* on the first section, *School choices* on the second and *Spare time choices* on the third. Ask the children to write, or draw with captions, the sorts of choices they make in each of these settings.

Ask the children to get into pairs and ask each other questions about the decisions they make.

Now ask them to look at their 'choices list' again and think about where they make most decisions – at home, at school or in their spare time. On a fresh sheet of paper ask them to write – or draw with captions – about a difficult decision they once had to make. The final sentence/line of their writing should be: 'this was a very hard decision for me to make because…'

Plenary
10 mins As a class, discuss the children's lists. Where do they make most decisions – at school, home or with their friends in their spare time? Where do they feel they have to make the hardest decisions – at home or school? Ask the children who they would talk to if they had a difficult choice or decision to make.

Differentiation
Younger and less able children may find it easier to concentrate on the decisions they make in one particular setting – at school for example. They can begin by listing the decisions they have to make at certain times of the school day, such as at lunch or playtimes. They can role play these scenarios with a small group.

Older and more able children can focus more on how to make more difficult decisions, such as whether or not to tell an adult about something they have seen

Making choices

others doing that they think is wrong. They may be able to write a set of simple guidance notes to help other children make difficult decisions. This could contain for example tips like, 'don't be too hasty', 'write down a list of all the pros and cons', 'share your concern with a friend' or 'ask a trusted adult for advice'.

Assessing learning outcomes
Can the children recognise the times in their daily lives when they have choices to make? Can they say what sorts of decisions they find hardest to make? Do the children understand that some decisions are more difficult to make than others and that sometimes it is sensible to ask the advice of people they trust?

① Are you a good consumer?
hour

Learning objectives
• Understand the effects of advertising on consumers.
• Develop strategies for making informed consumer decisions.

Lesson organisation
Whole-class, teacher-led introduction; individual work; plenary.

Vocabulary
consumer
advertising
publicity
persuasion
decisions
influence

What you need and preparation
Gather together a range of advertising material for everyday products that the children would see in shops or on television such as bicycles, computers games or confectionery. You will also need photocopiable page 137.

What to do

⑮ Introduction
mins
Show the children the collection of advertising material. Discuss how the advertisers and manufacturers have tried to convince consumers to buy their product. Can the children point out some of gimmicks that have been used? Do these gimmicks – such as a competition or free gifts – make them want to buy the product?

Can the children recall and recount a time when they begged their parents to buy them something they'd seen advertised on television? What kind of words have they used to create excitement about the product? What do the pictures make the children think of – hot, sunny beaches, daredevil acts, the best food in the world…? How many television advertisements can the children name? Which is the best one in their opinion? What makes it so good?

Make sure that the children understand that the purpose of advertisements is to persuade people to buy one product rather than another – to influence the choice of the consumer.

㉟ Development
mins
Explain to the children that they are going to look at how to make the best choice when buying something which costs a lot of money, for example a bicycle. Ask the children to work in pairs and give each pair a copy of photocopiable page 137. Tell the children to look carefully at the way the two bikes have been advertised.

First, ask the children make a list of questions they need to have answered before they can decide whether to buy either bike. For example, *How much does it cost? Is it the right size and weight? Is it suitable for the task?* – there's no point buying a racing bike with narrow tyres for cycling off road on rough terrain.

Now ask the children to look again at the adverts. What can they tell about the bikes from the advertisements? Do they provide the children with the answers to any of their questions they listed earlier? What is it impossible to know from the advertisements?

Ask the children to list three other ways of trying to decide whether or not to buy either of the bikes. For example they might write 'find out more about them', 'talk to my parents', 'decide what I need most from a mountain bike', 'compare the bikes with other bikes I've seen in another shop' or 'ask someone who already has a mountain bike'.

 Plenary
10 mins Discuss the children's ideas for making good consumer choices, and explain that as they get older they will have to make a lot more decisions about what to spend their money on, so learning how to make informed choices is a good skill to practise.

Differentiation
Older or more able children will be able to design advertising materials for a new product they have invented such as a kitchen gadget or a recycling machine. Alternatively, they could write new, more effective literature for an existing product they have often seen advertised.

Assessing learning outcomes
Can the children recognise how advertising literature works to influence their choices as consumers? Can the children see the importance of taking other factors into account before they buy something?

(1 hour) Is your time well spent?

What you need and preparation
Collect together some examples of timetables – school timetables, bus and train timetables and so on. You will also need photocopiable page 138.

What to do
Introduction
15 mins Ask the children to think about how they spend their time. Discuss with the children the different sorts of activities they are involved in during a normal week, for example going to school, doing homework, playing with friends, watching television, visiting relatives or going to a club. How do they fit all these activities into their lives and how do they make sure they get to the right place at the right time? Is there anything else the children wish they had time to do? What, apart from school, takes up most of their time?

Discuss the examples of timetables you have collected and make sure the children understand how they actually work. What do the columns and rows tell us? Compare the school timetable with a bus or train timetable and explain to the children that even though they give us very different sorts of information, they 'read' in the same way. Discuss why we have timetables and how they help us to manage our time.

Development
35 mins Give each child a copy of photocopiable page 138 and ask them to fill in the timetable showing how they could divide their time between all the things they have to do or would like to do. Explain to them that the suggestions in the box are examples of the sorts of activities that they might do during the week and that they can include others of their own in their timetables. Explain that they should try to account for as much of their time as possible. How will they spend their lunch breaks and what activities will they do after school and when?

Learning objectives
● Learn to make sensible informed choices about how to use time effectively.
● Understand that time management is an important part of building a healthy future.
● Learn to take responsibility for managing our time and organising ourselves.

Lesson organisation
Initial whole-class discussion; individual practice and reinforcement activity; short paired work session; plenary.

Vocabulary
time management
timetables
leisure time
commitments

Making choices

Plenary

10 mins Ask the children to compare their timetables with a friend. Which activities do they both do? Would it be possible to go to certain activities and places together? Would a friend be interested in joining a club to which their friend already belongs?

To round off the activity, discuss with the children which activities on their timetable can they choose and which they *must* do, for example going to school. How well do the children think they manage their time? Do they spend enough time exercising or playing with their friends? How many hours do they spend each week watching television or playing computer games? Suggest that the children take their timetables home to help them stay organised.

Differentiation

With younger and less able children it's a good idea to reinforce the concept of time management through 'story telling', for example by asking the children to tell you a story about something they have particularly enjoyed doing, including where and when they did it, with whom and why this particular activity was so enjoyable. They can then go on to think about what they like doing at the weekend and what they would most like to do if they had more time.

Older and more able children could add reminder notes to their timetables for example 'remember to take swimming kit'. They could also add a key indicating, for example, which activities they have a degree of choice over and which they are obliged to do.

Assessing learning outcomes

Do the children understand that managing their time involves a degree of choice, and that these choices are an important part of building a healthy future? Can the children recognise the difference between activities over which they have no control, such as attending school and those that allow a degree of choice, like choosing to stay in and read a book or go and play with a friend? Can the children map their regular time commitments and leisure pursuits onto a timetable and recognise that this should help them manage their time better?

ICT opportunity
Those children who are able to use a word processing facility quite fluently can create some spare timetables on the computer. This can then be printed out and used when children need to update or amend their original timetables – perhaps when they join a new club or take up a new hobby.

Follow-up activity
To help the children think about the sorts of commitments they may have to fit into their personal timetables in the future, they can make up a timetable for their parents/carers. What will they have to include (work, shopping, housework, taking children to school and to their activities, going to the gym and so on)?

Right or wrong?

What you need and preparation
You will need copies of photocopiable page 139.

What to do

15 mins Introduction
This activity focuses the children's attention on 'moral' issues and the role these play in citizenship. At this stage, the children can understand moral dilemmas and choices quite easily if they begin with their own experiences.

Introduce the idea of moral choices to the children by encouraging them to recall and relate a time when they were 'told off' by someone, usually an adult. What had they done wrong? Did they think it was fair to be told off for doing that particular thing? Why was it wrong?

Move the discussion along by asking the children to give you examples of other things that are generally considered to be wrong. Their suggestions will usually include things like stealing, bullying, killing people, vandalism and so on. Ask them to imagine what their local community or school would be like if, instead of being wrong, these things were considered to be right.

35 mins Development
Ask the children to work in pairs. Give each pair a copy of photocopiable page139. Ask the children to look at the scenario at the top of the sheet and to discuss what happens in the story. Do the children think that what the child did was right or wrong. Was it wrong to break the vase? (Not necessarily if it was an accident.) Now ask the children to look at the version of what happens next that is given on the sheet. Was it wrong to hide the fragments?

Now ask the children to draw an alternative version of what happens next where the child acts in a way that they think is morally more correct. Perhaps the child sweeps up the fragments, or perhaps she tells an adult about the broken vase.

Ask the children to come up with some similar scenarios of their own and draw or write further sets of 'moral dilemma' pictures. As a class, discuss the children's stories. Does everyone in the class agree with what is right and wrong?

10 mins Plenary
Compare and discuss the children's alternative versions and encourage them to explain why their versions show the 'right' course of action when a difficult moral choice has to be made – why is it better for example to own up to breaking dad's favourite wine glass?

Differentiation
Younger children will enjoy acting out the scenarios with a friend before they attempt the sheet. They could use puppets to role play their own 'right choices' scenes. In these ways the

Making choices

emphasis will remain on the issue of right and wrong, without the pressure of having to commit something to paper.

Older and more able children can carry out some research in the class or school library – how many stories can they find that have the theme of 'right and wrong?' These can include stories that have 'goodies and badies' as central characters such as *Peter Pan* or *Robin Hood*, *Little Red Riding Hood* and so on.

These children can also widen the focus by considering global rights and wrongs such as war, hunger and environmental issues such as pollution and global warming.

Assessing learning outcomes

Have the children understood that they have choices when it comes to making decisions about how to behave? Can the children explain why some activities and behaviour such as theft and bullying are thought by society to be wrong?

① What are our hopes and dreams?

**Learning
objectives**
• Examine the sorts
of choices they will
need to make as
they get older.
• Think about what
they might like to
do when there are
older and what
they will have to do
in order to achieve
their hopes and
dreams.

**Lesson
organisation**
Introductory
whole-class
discussion; group
work; plenary.

Vocabulary
hopes
dreams
ambitions
plans
future

What you need

Gather together a selection of reference books about growing up.

What to do

⑩ Introduction

To introduce the idea of making choices in the future, ask the children what sorts of things their parents/carers have to do because they are adults but that the children do not have to do, for example going to work, cooking, shopping, looking after children, organising the household and so on. List these on the board or a flip chart.

Ask the children what kinds of choices they will have to make as they get older, for example which exams to take, what sort of job to do, where to live, whether to get married and have children and so on. What would be their dream lifestyle?

⑳ Development

Explain to the children that you would like them to make a class book called 'Hopes and dreams' (or choose another title if you prefer). Ask the children to work in groups and give each group a different stage of life to focus on. Explain to the children that each group should work on ideas for what they think they will be doing – or what they hope to be doing – at that stage in their life.

● *Group 1* Produce a chapter of two or three pages (depending on the size of the group) for the class book called 'When I'm nine'. Write and illustrate the hopes, dreams or plans.
● *Group 2* Produce the chapter called 'When I leave school…'
● *Group 3* Produce the chapter called 'When I am the same age as my parents…'
● *Group 4* Prepare the final chapter called 'When I'm as old as my grandparents…'

When each section is finished they can be gathered together to make a complete book. You may not be able to complete the whole book in this time, but the children should aim to finish a draft during this first session.

⑩ Plenary

Share and discuss the ideas produced so far by the three groups and recap on the kinds of things the children will need to do if they are to achieve their hopes and dreams, for example get good qualifications, understand what they're good at and not so good at, get a job that will make them happy and pay well and so on.

Discuss as a class how to proceed with making the book. Would they like to use the computer to redraft the text or design a cover?

Differentiation

Generally the younger children will find it easier to imagine what they might be doing in one or two rather than 20 or 30 years' time. This age group can also add a final page – perhaps as a drawing about their dream job.

Older and more able children can find out more about some of the ideas they have for the future, for example what qualifications they will need for the job they think they would enjoy most, or what life is like in the foreign country they would like to live in. These children can also add further chapters depicting their hopes, dreams and plans, for example when they are 25 or 30 years old.

Assessing learning outcomes

Can the children identify the kinds of choices they will have to make as they get older? Can the children describe their hopes and dreams for the future and begin to reflect on what they will need to do to achieve them?

> **ICT opportunities**
> • The children can use a desktop publishing programme to redraft text for the class book and design a cover.
> • The children could search the Internet for further information on the ideas they have written about, for example on occupations or countries.
> • The children could also make a taped version of their finished book for someone who has impaired vision.

> **Follow up activity**
> In subsequent sessions – perhaps as part of your Literacy Hour activities – the children could work on their drafts and work together to complete the class book.

Sustainable development

Sustainable development refers to the effective management of resources to ensure that societies can continue to function efficiently in the future. It follows therefore that children – as the future custodians of the world's natural resources – should be taught how to manage them.

Sustainable development raises questions such as: can the environment continue to provide resources at this level? What happens when resources such as oil or coal run out? What impact does our current level of resource use have on environmental factors such as the ozone layer, deforestation, climate change and third world debt? How can alternative technology help with sustainable development?

The sustainable development themes introduced in this unit are:

● **the effect of out of town shopping complexes on sustainable development**

The children are invited to express their views – based on practical investigations – on whether it would be a good or a bad thing for the community if a huge, new hypermarket was built on the outskirts of town. The activity asks them to consider the impact such a development would have on local traffic, local shopkeepers and residents.

● **alternative technology**

The theme of alternative technology is explored through asking the children to design their ideal home using only renewable resources.

● **technological development into the future**

We are living in an age of huge and rapid technological development, and it will be essential for the children to learn how to manage technology in their everyday lives. The activity asks them to reflect on whether all the technology and digital gadgets they have around them are strictly necessary – how much will survive into the future?

● **renewable and non-renewable resources**

The final activity is a board game that is designed to reinforce, in a fun way, the main issues relating to sustainable development.

UNIT: Sustainable development

Enquiry questions	Learning objectives	Teaching activities	Learning outcomes	Cross-curricular links
Out-of-town – out of reach?	• Reflect on the impact of out-of-town shopping centres on sustainable development. • Compare local facilities to those offered by shopping centres.	Discussion about shopping habits. Pair work to discover the pros and cons of shopping centres. Reach a decision about whether to allow such a development.	*Children:* • explain the advantages and disadvantages of shopping centres • understand their environmental impact	Geography: investigating local environments.
What are the alternatives?	• Understand the importance of managing resources. • Make the link between resource management and sustainability. • Investigate sources of alternative energy and reflect on the use of renewable resources.	Work through a photocopiable sheet to identify the features of an environmentally friendly house.	• recognise sustainable processes and materials • say why these are important for the future	Science: materials and their properties. Geography: conservation.
Technology – where will we be in the future?	• Investigate modern technology. • Consider if the current rates of technological development are necessary and sustainable.	Investigate which technologies they use in different situations. Work towards an understanding through writing of which technology is essential.	• understand the part technology plays in our lives • make the connection between technology and sustainability	ICT: identify a range of technologies and know how they help us.
What is man-made?	• Learn about natural and man-made materials. • Find out about renewable and non-renewable resources.	Teacher leads children through a classification exercise. Research different materials and resources.	• make the connection between non-renewable resources and sustainability • classify materials and resources	Science: materials and their properties; classification.
Are we on the right track?	• Reflect on issues relating to sustainable development.	Play a board game.	• recognise why the snake spaces are examples of bad environmental habits.	

Resources
A local map showing a radius of 5 miles from the town/ciy, reference books about supermarkets and out-of-town shopping centres, an overhead projector, reference materials about alternative technologies, a selection of everyday objects made from a range of manufactured and natural materials.

Display
Photographs of deserted town centres, car parks and traffic jams.

CHAPTER 5
BUILDING A HEALTHY
FUTURE

Sustainable
development

Learning objectives
• Reflect on the implications that out-of-town shopping centres have for long-term development and sustainability.
• Compare and contrast the facilities offered by local and out-of-town centres.

Lesson organisation
Initial whole-class discussion; paired work; plenary.

Vocabulary
supermarkets
hypermarkets
out-of-town shopping centres
parking
transport
local community

What you need and preparation
A local map showing a radius of around 5 miles from the local town or city centre. Gather together some reference books about supermarkets and out-of-town shopping centres. Photographs or magazine pictures of large shops, deserted town centres and empty shops, car parks and traffic jams. Any historical evidence you can find about the town or city centre as it was say 20–50 years ago. You will need access to an overhead projector. Make copies of photocopiable page 140

What to do

15 mins Introduction
Begin by asking the children where their parents/carers usually do their shopping – in local shops (those in the centre of the town, city or village where they live), in supermarkets some way out of town or in a really big hypermarket several miles out of town? To help the children work this out, ask them if they need a car or bus to get there and roughly how long it takes.

Share the reference material with the class and discuss the reasons why people may prefer to shop in a large supermarket as opposed to in lots of different shops. What are the advantages of shopping locally? What do the children think would happen to their local town centre if everyone shopped out of town? What effects would this have on the people who lived and worked there?

If you have photographic evidence of the history of your local town centre, discuss this with the children asking them to look carefully at the changes that have occurred. Why do they think these changes have happened?

On the overhead projector, show the children the map of the local area and plot on the map with them the locations of local shopping centres, out-of-town supermarkets and hypermarkets.

20 mins Development
Working in pairs, tell the children that they are going to be planners trying to decide whether or not to allow a huge hypermarket to be built 5 miles outside of their local town. Give each pair a copy of photocopiable page 140 and explain that they have to list as many good and bad points as they can think of. They should think especially carefully about the environmental issues such as traffic, loss of green spaces and so on.

15 mins Plenary
Discuss the children's lists and ask each pair if overall it would be a good or a bad thing for the hypermarket to be built. What effects will it have on the local environment (more traffic

jams, exhaust fumes, loss of green land and habitats for wildlife and so on)? What will it mean for the people who live and work locally (job losses, difficulties for people without transport, people may move out of the area, more traffic on the roads and so on)? How are people going to get there?

Carry out a class vote by show of hands to see if the children think the huge new shop should or should not be built.

Differentiation

Younger children will find it easier to relate to this topic if they first talk about, or act out, stories about shopping trips they have been on with their families. How did they feel – was it exciting to be in a huge shop or was it boring and tiring? Can they remember going into a local shop to buy something and having a chat with the shopkeeper? These children will also need extra support with map reading and plotting where shops are located.

Older and more able children can extend their work by writing letters as if from the Managing Director of the company wanting to build the hypermarket to the local planning department. This letter should set out the advantages such a shop would have for local residents and the environment.

Assessing learning outcomes

Can the children describe the main environmental issues relating to the development of out-of-town shopping complexes? Can they reflect on the effects that a hypermarket built out-of-town would have on the future of the local community and its environment? Can they give considered reasons for and against a specific issue and listen to the views and ideas of others who may not agree with them?

> **Follow-up activity**
> The ideas and issues contained in this activity can be enhanced by inviting a local shopkeeper or older member of the community in to talk to the class about their first-hand experiences and the changes they have seen in the way people shop.

What are the alternatives?

What you need

Gather together a selection of resource books and resources on alternative technology, energy and 'green buildings'. Collect together photographs, magazine or newspaper pictures of buildings showing alternative technologies such as wind power, solar panels, insulation materials and so on. You will also need photocopiable page 141.

What to do

Introduction
10 mins Discuss the pictures and resource books with the children making sure they understand the environmental issues involved. Ask them to tell you what they know about things like windmills, recycling plants, solar heating and so on.

Development
45 mins Tell the children that they are going to be planners and architects of the future and their job is to build an ideal home for a family using as many environmentally friendly materials and processes as they can. They are allowed to invent their own green technologies as long as they can explain their advantages to the environment.

Ask the children to work in pairs and give each pair a copy of photocopiable page 141. Make sure they understand that they must use some of the environmentally friendly materials and processes given on the sheet. They should use the resources provided and the Internet if

> **Learning objectives**
> • Consider how the resources necessary to sustain communities in the future need to be managed.
> • Investigate sources of alternative energy and reflect on the use of renewable resources.
>
> **Lesson organisation**
> Introductory whole class, teacher-led discussion; paired follow-up work; plenary.

Sustainable development

possible to give them further ideas and information.

Plenary
15 mins Ask the children to share and compare ideas. How many of the 'green' materials and processes have they used in their ideal design? Has anybody come up with a brilliant new idea for saving or managing resources? Have any of their homes got these things already?

Differentiation
Younger and less able children may find it easier to work with only one or two of the ideas. For example, they could show how household litter could be re-used or how the family would save water in an ideal home of the future. They can write and illustrate stories about their ideal home and what is so special about it.

Older and more able children can begin to look at scale in their plans and give some rough measurements, for example, 'solar heated bathroom 6m by 4m'. They can also go on to find out more about the technologies and materials given on the sheet.

Assessing learning outcomes
Can the children recognise materials and processes that are sustainable into the future? Can they see how such materials and processes can be used to make homes of the future more environmentally sound? Can they explain why using renewable resources is an important part of building a healthy future?

40 mins Technology – where will we be in the future?

What you need and preparation
Photocopiable page 142. Reference resources on modern machines and technology such as computers, satellite dishes and cash machines. Writing materials.

What to do
Introduction
10 mins Write the word *technology* on the board or on a flip chart and ask the children what it means (machines and processes that help us to carry out common

place activities more quickly – especially those that use digital or microchip technology like computers, calculators, e-mail and remote controls). Ask them to name as many of these 'hi-tech' items as they can think of (CDs, digital watches, fax machines, mobile telephones, satellite dishes, DVD players and so on). How do these things help us? What role does technology play in our lives? How did people manage before they were invented?

Development
20 mins Give each child a copy of photocopiable page 142 and discuss the list of hi-tech items on the sheet. Do the children know what they all are?

How many of these do they use regularly? Ask the children to record on the sheet where these items are used, for example under *Home* they would write 'television, telephone, video' and so on. They will find that some of the items are used at school as well as at home such as a calculator and computer; some items will be used in all three places. Once the children have their lists ask them to put a green circle round the three items they consider to be the most useful, and a red circle round the three they think they could most easily do without.

Now ask the children to write a story or short sketch about a time when a piece of technology saved them from disaster (this can be a true-life or imaginary experience). For example, using a mobile phone to help them when they were lost or medical technology helping them when they were ill.

 Plenary
Compare and discuss the items and technology that individual children have decided are the most important and ask them to say why they chose them. Do the same for the things children have identified as being dispensable. Talk about what happens to all the machinery and gadgets that nobody wants anymore. As computer technology advances so rapidly for example, people don't want to buy second-hand machines and so the old ones are wasted. Where does it all go? Can they be recycled?

Differentiation
Older or more able children can take this idea further by investigating what materials are used to make computers, satellite dishes and so on and look at the impact on the environment.

Assessing learning outcomes
Do the children understand the part technology plays in their lives? Can they make sensible judgements about which technologies have become crucial to communities? Do the children understand the links between technology and sustainable development, for example do they recognise that developments in technology have a cost to the environment?

> **Follow-up activity**
> The children can use the technological words given on the sheet, and add any others they can think of, to make a word search puzzle for a friend to solve.

What is man-made?

What you need and preparation
Gather together a selection of everyday objects made from a range of manufactured and natural materials, for example, wooden/plastic rulers, an aluminium tray from a fast food outlet, a paper cup, scissors, a mixed-fibre sweater and so on. Collect together reference books on materials and fabrics. You will also need two hoops from the PE store and photocopiable sheet 143.

What to do
Introduction
Place the two hoops flat, but slightly overlapping, on a large table and label them *Manufactured* and *Natural*. Discuss the collection of everyday objects with the children and ask them to name the materials they are made from. Ask them to help you to classify the objects into sets by placing them in the hoops according to whether they are made from synthetic or manufactured materials or from natural ones. What about those that are made from a mixture of both? Where will they place those?

Talk to the children about where the materials for these objects come from (paper from

> **Learning objectives**
> ● Identify which everyday objects are made from natural material and which are artificial or manufactured.
> ● Learn about renewable and non-renewable resources and what the use of these resources means for the long-term future.

> **Lesson organisation**
> Whole-class introduction; individual or paired reinforcement activity; plenary.

Sustainable development

Vocabulary
resources
renewable
non-renewable
sustainability
man-made
natural

trees, plastics from oil, glass from sand and so on). Explain to the children that some of these materials come from non-renewable resources, for example some hardwoods are from rainforest trees that are hundreds of years old, and plastics are made from oil which, once it has all gone, cannot be replaced (non-renewable). Develop the children's understanding further by repeating the classification activity, this time looking at the sources of the materials. Rename the hoops *Renewable* and *Non-renewable*.

35 mins Development
Ask the children to work in pairs and give each pair a copy of photocopiable page 143. Explain to the children that they should investigate the materials listed on the sheet and should try to answer the questions on the sheet. They should be encouraged to use the reference books to find out further information about the materials that they are asked to classify and discuss.

10 mins Plenary
Ask the children to share and discuss the results of their investigations, and revisit the objects they helped you classify at the beginning. Ask for volunteers to say a sentence about one of the objects using the information from their investigations, for example, 'this paper cup is made from trees that are grown specially for making paper', or 'this plastic ruler is made from oil, which is a non-renewable resource'.

Differentiation
The younger or less able children will find it easier to work for longer with the real objects before they attempt to find out more from reference sources. They can make labels for the different objects in each of the two sets, for example 'this is made of paper, paper is made from trees'.

For older and more able children the concept of sorting and classifying material can be reinforced by asking them to draw Venn diagrams. These children could also write or send an e-mail to the Centre for Alternative Technology in Wales asking for more information about sustainable technology and conservation of resources.

Assessing learning outcomes
Can the children identify which everyday objects are made from materials that are renewable or non-renewable? Do the children understand the links between non-renewable resources and a sustainable environment?

(35 mins) Are we on the right track?

What you need and preparation

Enlarge photocopiable page 144 and make enough copies for the children to have one between three. You will also need a counter for each player and enough dice for each group of players to have one.

What to do

(10 mins) Introduction

Remind the children what we mean by sustainability. Can they come up with a catch-phrase or jingle to describe the importance of sustainable development, such as 'use it all today, there'll be none left for tomorrow'. Ask the children to work in groups of three and give each group a copy of photocopiable page 144. Explain to the children that they are going to be playing the 'Sustainability game', which is a version of 'Snakes and Ladders'.

(20 mins) Development

Briefly recap on the rules of the game: each player must throw a six to start; the winner is the first player to land on the *Future* space. Encourage the children to read out the squares as they land on them and to think about why each action is good or bad for sustaining our environment so that we have enough resources for the future.

(5 mins) Plenary

Discuss the action squares on the 'Sustainablity game' board. Ask the children to explain why each action is significant for the future of the environment and the people who will live in it. Invite them to suggest other sustainability themes for the squares on the board.

Differentiation

Younger and less able readers may need some help with the words on the board. They may need guidance in making the connections between the environmental issues raised. For a younger player, you could suspend the rule that requires them to throw a six to start.

Older and more able players can adapt the rules. For example, they might decide to play with two dice, or take two from the number thrown if it is an even number and subtract one from all odd numbers thrown. They could keep a tally of the number of times they land on snakes or ladders and work out averages and so on.

Assessing learning outcomes

Do the children enjoy playing the game? Do they understand why the spaces containing snakes and ladders are about issues that threaten the future well-being of the environment?

Learning objectives
• Reflect on issues relating to sustainable development.

Lesson organisation
Short introductory session to explain the game to the class; game in small groups; plenary.

Vocabulary
hardwoods
aluminium
managed forests
recycled materials

Follow-up activity
Get the children to create their own version of a sustainability game. They could either write new issues for the snakes and ladders spaces or they could adapt another favourite game.

Name _____ Date _____

Who am I?

Fill in the missing words below to create a poem about yourself.

I'm the sort of person who likes to _____

I'm the sort of person who hates to _____

Happiness for me is _____

Frightening for me is _____

I'm the sort of person who imagines _____

I'm the sort of person who wants _____

I dream that one day I'll _____

But for now I'm just _____

Now try writing a stanza about a member of your family. Use the back of this sheet.

Name _____   Date _____

All about me

Name_____

Age_____ Years_____ Months_____

Class_____ Date_____

School _____

Favourite subjects_____

_____

I was proud of myself when I _____

_____

When I'm not at school, I like to_____

_____

What I'm good at _____

_____

Things that I could improve on_____

_____

Signature_____

Name _____   Date _____

Are you tickled pink?

How do you think these children are feeling? How can you tell?

Name _____   Date _____

The Jabberwocky

'Twas brillig, and the slithy toves
Did gyre and gimble in the wabe:
All mimsy were the borogroves,
And the mome raths outgrabe.

"Beware the Jabberwock, my son!
The jaws that bite, the claws that catch!
Beware the Jujub bird, and shun
The frumious Bandersnatch!"

He took his vorpal sword in hand:
Long time the manxome foe he sought–
So rested he by the Tumtum tree,
And stood awhile in thought.

And, as in uffish thought he stood,
The Jabberwock, with eyes of flame,
Came whiffling through the tulgey wood,
And burbled as it came!

One, two! One, two! And through and through
The vorpal blade went snicker-snack!
He left it dead, and with its head
he went galumphing back.

"And hast thou slain the Jabberwock?
Come to my arm, my beamish boy!
O frabjous day! Callooh! Callay!"
He chortled in his joy.

'Twas brillig, and the slithy toves
Did gyre and gimble in the wabe:
All mimsy were the borogroves,
And the mome raths outgrabe.

by Lewis Carroll

PHOTOCOPIABLE

Name _____   Date _____

Has anybody seen the green-eyed monster?

She's **my** friend.

I want one, too!

PRIMARY FOUNDATIONS: PSHE: Ages 7–9

Name _____   Date _____

Are you eating a healthy diet?

List as many foods as you can under the four food groups

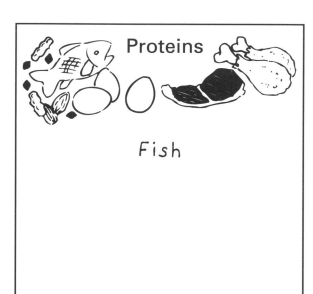

Proteins

Fish

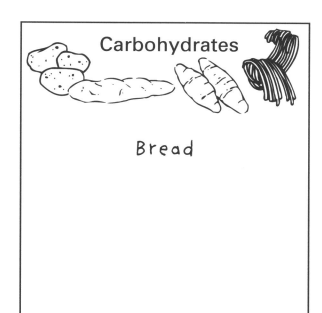

Carbohydrates

Bread

Dairy products

Cheese

Fruit and vegetables

Apple

Name _____   Date _____

Is this recipe good for you?

Chocolate flake cake

For the cake:

25g cocoa powder

1 tsp baking powder

150g self-raising flour

150g margarine or butter

150g caster sugar

3 eggs

To serve:

50g dark chocolate

25g butter

110g icing sugar

150ml double cream

2 flakes

a few fresh raspberries

Carrot and pineapple bran muffins

1 cup boiling water

1 cup natural bran

1 egg

1/3 cup brown sugar

½ cup shredded carrot

½ cup unsweetened crushed pineapple

2 tablespoons vegetable oil

1 cup plain flour

1/3 cup milk powder

1 ½ tsps bicarbonate of soda

½ tsp ground ginger

Which recipe has the healthiest ingredients?_____

Why?_____

_____

BUILDING HEALTHY BODIES: **Eating well**
What's in a snack? Page 38

PHOTOCOPIABLE

Name _____   Date _____

What's in a snack?

Fill in the boxes for these snacks. The first one has been done for you. In the boxes at the bottom, record the details of the two wrappers you have been given.

Snack food	What's in it?	What other more healthy sources are there for these foods?
Packet of crisps	Potatoes Oil salt	Baked/boiled potatoes Olive oil Natural salt in vegetables
Chocolate bar		
Fizzy drink		
Wrapper 1		
Wrapper 2		

Name _____   Date _____

Exercise – how much is enough?

Use this timetable to plan your week's exercise and activities. Sunday has been done for you – but you can change it if you like.

	Morning	Lunchtime	Afternoon	Evening
Sunday	Play football	Cycle to the shop to buy milk	Go for a walk with my Dad	Take the dog for a walk
Monday				
Tuesday				
Wednesday				
Thursday				
Friday				
Saturday				

Name _____   Date _____

Exercise – the golden rules

Fill in the 'golden' dos and don'ts of exercise.

Use these statements to get you started	Always	Never
Start sprinting straightaway.		
Stretch your muscles first.		
Eat a big pile of greasy food just before you exercise.		
Cool down your muscles after vigorous exercise.		
Wear dangly jewellery.		
Drink water after exercise.		

PHOTOCOPIABLE

BUILDING HEALTHY BODIES: Keeping fit
Can you invent your own games? Page 49

Name _____   Date _____

Invent your own game

Name of game					How is it played?		Rules	How is it good for your:
Equipment used 							1.	Heart
							2.	Lungs
When is it played?							3.	Muscles
Summer		Winter			How is a point scored?		4.	
Where is it played?							5.	Co-ordination

PRIMARY FOUNDATIONS: PSHE: Ages 7–9

Name _____   Date _____

A game for everyone

How would a disabled person benefit from the game?		
Rules		
How is it played?		**How is a point scored?**
Name of game		
Equipment used		
When is it played?	Summer ☀ Winter	
Where is it played?		

Name _____   Date _____

What is waste?

How do these everyday activities make waste?

	What waste does this make?	How does this damage the environment?	How can we reduce the waste?

Use these words to get you started:

litter   organic materials   acid rain

fire smoke   electricity generators   sewage   fumes

Name _____   Date _____

What's under wraps?

How environmentally friendly are these containers? Can you answer the questions below? The first one has been done for you.

Packaging	🍾 Bottle	🥫 Can	📦 Carton
Is it heavy?	✔	✘	✘
Does it take up space?			
Is it easily crushed?			
Can it be recycled?			
Can it be burned to recover the energy used to make it?			
What are its good points?			
What are its bad points?			
What is your overall summary of the container?			
Which container is the best to use? Why?			

PHOTOCOPIABLE

BUILDING HEALTHY ENVIRONMENTS: Waste not want not
Are we awash with water? Page 58

Name _____   Date_____

Are we awash with water?

Use this vocabulary to fill in the boxes on this diagram of the water cycle.

clouds	river	lake	stream
estuary	sea	evaporates	
condenses	rain	ground	

Name _____   Date _____

Saving water the easy way

Look at the pictures in the four boxes. Think about how much water they use. Write your ideas about how to save water.

I can save water by…

_____

_____

_____

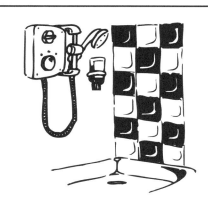

I can save water by…

_____

_____

_____

I can save water by…

_____

_____

_____

I can save water by…

_____

_____

_____

Name _____   Date _____

What is pollution?

Can you write three examples of each type of pollution:

Sound pollution

1. Loud music _____

2. _____

3. _____

Air pollution

1. _____

2. _____

3. _____

Water pollution

1. _____

2. _____

3. _____

Name _____   Date _____

What do we know about wildlife?

Vocabulary

environment

wildlife park

conservation

endangered species

habitats

advantages

disadvantages

How do zoos and wildlife parks help endangered species?

_____

_____

_____

I think zoos and wildlife parks are a good thing because...

_____

_____

_____

I think they are a bad thing because...

_____

_____

_____

Name _____   Date _____

Living on the fence

Use this sheet to record what you have found in your fence, hedge or wall.

Fences	Hedges	Railings	Walls

PRIMARY FOUNDATIONS: PSHE: Ages 7–9

Name _____   Date _____

Who makes things happen around here?

Who works in our community? Fill in the columns below.

Daytime jobs	Night-time jobs	Day and night jobs

PHOTOCOPIABLE

BUILDING HEALTHY COMMUNITIES: Working together
Who makes things happen around here? Page 75

Name _____   Date _____

Which jobs are important in our community?

Find out about a job that is important to your local community.
Record your findings here:

Job title _____

_____

How does this job help the community?_____

_____

_____

Describe a day in the life of someone who does this job.

_____

_____

How can we help this person do their job for the community?

_____

_____

Name _____   Date _____

Even desert islands need rules!

Your class has been stranded on a desert island. What rules will you create to help you live together on the island until you are rescued?

You might want rules about:

Chores
Crimes
Safety
Leaders

How would you make sure people stuck to the rules?

1. _____

2. _____

3. _____

4. _____

5. _____

BUILDING HEALTHY COMMUNITIES: **Working together**

What's the shopping centre all about? Page 78

PHOTOCOPIABLE

Name _____   Date _____

What's at the shopping centre?

What shops and services have you found at the local shopping centre?

Shops	Repairs and services	Food outlets	Other businesses

PHOTOCOPIABLE

Name _____   Date _____

Is our school a community too?

Think about the different sorts of groups that make up your school community. Fill in the missing groups on the diagram below, and say what each group is responsible for. The first one has been done for you.

_____

Responsible for:

_____

_____

_____

_____

Responsible for:

_____

_____

_____

Our school community

_____

Responsible for:

_____

_____

_____

_____

Responsible for:

_____

_____

_____

Name _____   Date _____

Does your vote count?

Polling card for children to fill in:

✂ --

NAME: _____   REF: _____

ADDRESS: _____

_____

_____

CLASS ELECTION
OFFICIAL POLLING CARD

- -

NAME: _____   REF: _____

ADDRESS: _____

_____

_____

CLASS ELECTION
OFFICIAL POLLING CARD

Name _____   Date _____

What do we need in our community?

Name of community group	

What facilities do this group need?	Are they provided?	How can you find out?	What can you do to help?
1.			
2.			
3.			
4.			

BUILDING HEALTHY COMMUNITIES: Something for everyone
What do we do about greed? Page 88
PHOTOCOPIABLE

Name _____   Date _____

What can we do about greed?

Look at the two situations. Draw what you think happened next?
Can you add a caption to your drawing?

Name _____   Date _____

Are you part of the community?

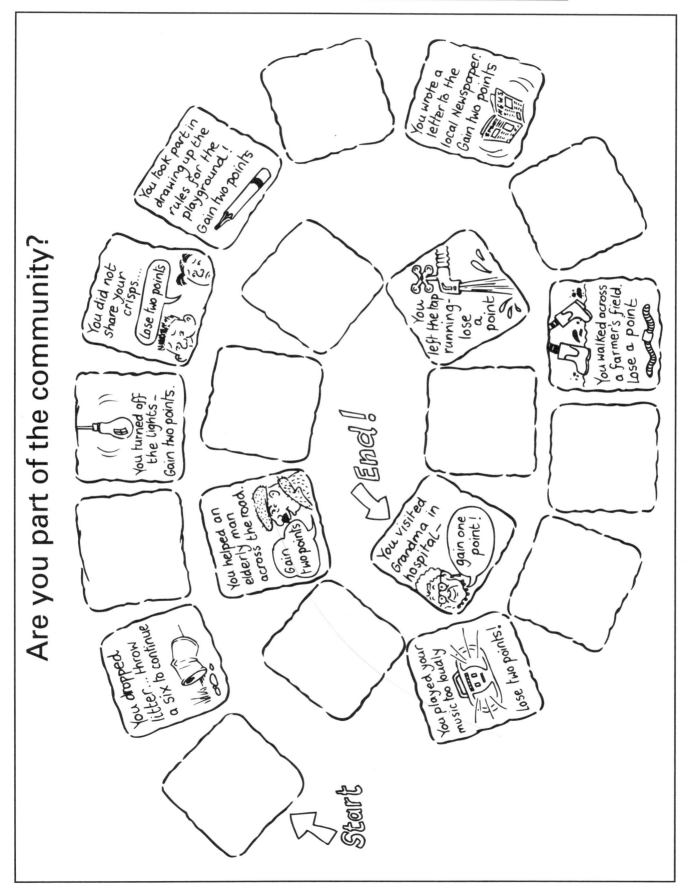

PHOTOCOPIABLE

BUILDING HEALTHY COMMUNITIES: Something for everyone
Are we part of the community? Page 89

Name _____   Date _____

Are you part of the community?

SCORE SHEET

Name of players   Player 1 _____

Player 2 _____

Game 1		Game 2		Game 3		Game 4	
Player 1	Player 2	Player 1	Player 2	Player 1	Player 2	Player 1	Player 2

TOTALS

Name _____   Date _____

Are you a good consumer?

Look at the adverts below. Which bike would you like to buy? How are you going to decide?

How will you decide which bike to buy?

1. _____

2. _____

3. _____

4. _____

5. _____

PHOTOCOPIABLE

BUILDING A HEALTHY FUTURE: Making choices
Is your time well spent? Page 95

Name _____   Date _____

Is your time well spent?

Fill in how much time you could spend on your activities. Monday has been done for you.

Activity	Monday	Tuesday	Wednesday	Thursday	Friday	Saturday	Sunday
Reading	30 mins						
Playing computer games	20 mins						
Playing with friends	1 hour						
Homework	30 mins						
Eating	1 hour						
Helping around the house/ garden	20 mins						
Watching television	1 hour						
Hobbies	1 hour						
After-school activities	1 hour						
Others (fill in):							

PHOTOCOPIABLE

Name _____ Date _____

Right or wrong?

PHOTOCOPIABLE

Name _____ Date _____

Out of town – out of reach?

There are plans for a new out-of-town superstore. Are you for it or against it?

Vocabulary

- Traffic
- Parking
- Loss of green areas
- Loss of jobs
- Noise for people living nearby
- Community
- Resources
- Development

Yes, I'm in favour of a new superstore because:

1. _____

_____

2. _____

_____

3. _____

_____

No, I'm against the superstore because:

1. _____

_____

2. _____

_____

3. _____

_____

140

BUILDING A HEALTHY FUTURE: **Sustainable development**
What are the alternatives? Page 103

PHOTOCOPIABLE

Name _____   Date _____

A green house

This family lives in an environmentally friendly house. Look at each of the rooms and say how they have used natural resources well in each room to make sure their house doesn't use up too many resources.

Use these words to help you.

- Recycled water
- Reed bed filtration system
- Solar energy
- Insulation
- Renewable resources
- Waste
- Wildlife
- Flora
- Fauna

PHOTOCOPIABLE

BUILDING A HEALTHY FUTURE: **Sustainable development**
Technology – where will we be in the future? Page 104

Name _____   Date _____

Technology for the future

What technology do you use? Make a list under each heading of the types of technology we use in these places.

You might be using:	Home	School	Community
Remote control			
Digital timers			
Computers			
E-mail			
Internet			
Television			
Radio			
Satellite			
Telephone			
Mobile phone			
Cash machine			
Camera			
Modem			
Video			
CD-ROMs			
CCTV			

Name _____   Date _____

Manufactured or natural?

- Find out about the following materials.
- Record your findings on the table below.

	Where does it come from?	Is it a renewable resource?	Can you recycle it?
Wood			
Plastic			
Cotton			
Aluminium			
Glass			
Polystyrene			

Name _____   Date _____

Are we on the right track?

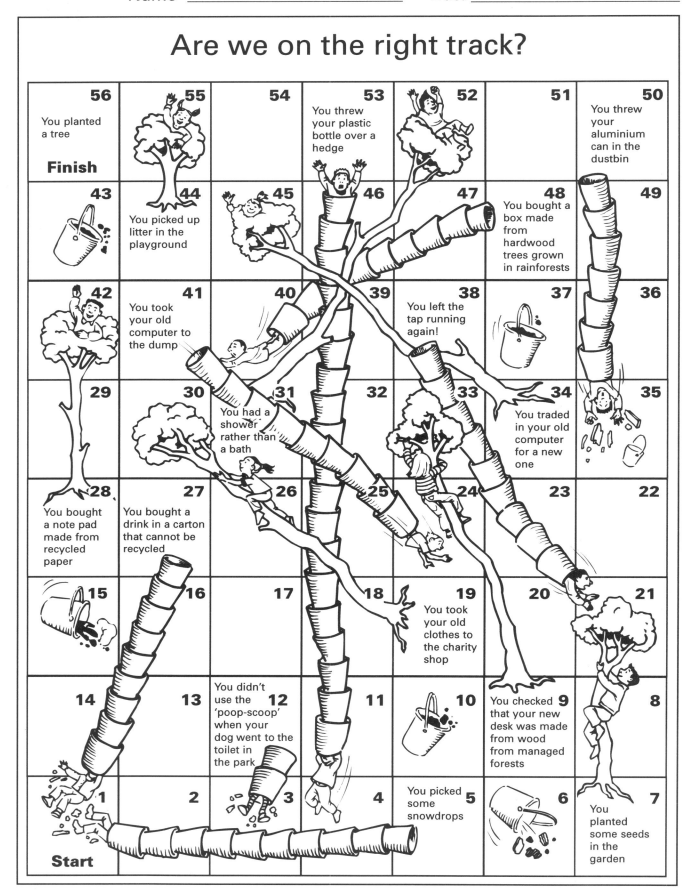

56 You planted a tree **Finish**

55

54

53 You threw your plastic bottle over a hedge

52

51

50 You threw your aluminium can in the dustbin

43

44 You picked up litter in the playground

45

46

47

48 You bought a box made from hardwood trees grown in rainforests

49

42

41 You took your old computer to the dump

40

39

38 You left the tap running again!

37

36

29

30

31 You had a shower rather than a bath

32

33

34 You traded in your old computer for a new one

35

28 You bought a note pad made from recycled paper

27 You bought a drink in a carton that cannot be recycled

26

25

24

23

22

15

16

17

18

19 You took your old clothes to the charity shop

20

21

14

13

12 You didn't use the 'poop-scoop' when your dog went to the toilet in the park

11

10

9 You checked that your new desk was made from wood from managed forests

8

1

2

3

4

5 You picked some snowdrops

6

7 You planted some seeds in the garden

Start